THIS
IS
THAT

How to see the Kingdom of Heaven in everyday living

Martin J. Young

malcolm down

PUBLISHING

First published 2021 by Malcolm Down Publishing Ltd.
www.malcolmdown.co.uk

24 23 22 21 20   7 6 5 4 3 2 1

British Library Cataloguing in Publication Data
A catalogue record for this book is available from the British Library.

ISBN 978-1-912863-40-2

Original cover art by Jon White
www.jonwhite.com
Cover design by Andrew Pressdee
Art direction by Sarah Grace

Printed in the UK

Endorsements

This is a book for thinkers, for dreamers and for those who know the world can heal and be restored, if we will adhere more closely to the Kingdom of God and do what we can to emulate His love and grace, despite and because of the brokenness of our world. As Martin so cogently states, the imprint of God has not been wiped from us despite the corruption and abuse the earth and its peoples have suffered at the hands of those called to nurture it. It is delight in the Creator which forms the deeply fulfilling labour of the first Kingdom mandate. In reading this beautifully expressed hope for better things, Martin Young displays the heart of God's Kingdom. Read it and you will be changed, I guarantee it.

Bev Murrill, Founder of Kyria Leaders Network, Liberti Magazine and co-founder of CGI church network

This book is a beautiful poetic portrait of the Kingdom of God through lived experience in Martin's life and ministry. It's a collage of thought, participation, imagination, and wisdom. If you think you've got a handle on what the kingdom of God is all about then read this book, it will explode that neat box you've made. Love it.

Roger Sutton, Leader of the GATHER collaboration and Movement Day UK and chairman of the Trafford Council Strategic Partnership

I appreciate how Martin has approached the essence of the Kingdom in a different way. The re-imagination of shalom, the wholeness of our world, through the eyes of culture and design, is really impactful.

Nigel Langford, Head of church relations at the Bible Society

Martin wrote this book before the outbreak of COVID-19 but as it approaches being published we find ourselves yearning for the Kingdom of God more than ever. Martin writes 'The Kingdom of Heaven, being experienced and lived out on this earth, was always God's plan for humanity and is also what the story and teaching of the Bible is about'.

It was always God's intention but are we seeing the church waking up to its reality more and more? This book gives us hope for that and pushes us towards it.

Debra Green OBE, Founder and CEO of ROC

Martin invites us to take a journey through the bible as he underlines the persistent and consistent thread of the Kingdom of Heaven on earth. He explores timeless truths and deep wisdom, unlocking familiar passages in creative, imaginative and even playful ways. Come to this book with an open heart and mind. Expect to be moved and challenged. Expect your vision and passion for more of the Kingdom of Heaven in your life and on your piece of earth, to be powerfully reignited.

Cham Kaur Mann, Co-director of Next Leadership

Contents

Part 3: Jesus and the Kingdom of Heaven

Part 4: Prophets, Priests and Kings

Part 5: God-Pointing

I would like to dedicate the book to my parents:

This book is written in honour of my parents, David and Joy Young, who lived with a great appreciation of life to the full, in science, literature, music, colour, creation, hospitality and people; shared their faith with commitment and kindness; and enjoyed the freedom of keeping their eyes on the city coming down from heaven.

The Kingdom of Heaven

The Kingdom of God is *it*. It's what we are all longing for, deep down: every human being on the planet. It is the way that we were always meant to live, our default culture. This Kingdom of Heaven has always been the number one plan for the earth and its inhabitants – birds, fish, animals and people. It is like a code or rhythm or set of musical motifs established a very long time ago, to which humanity and the whole of creation would live and move and have its being. The Kingdom is the call of the King: the song of the King, the breath of the King, the words, thoughts and actions of the King; in harmony with the many varied response of everything that the King has made.

For many of us, we don't just yearn for something better, away from this existence: we look for this one to be packed full of goodness and satisfaction. Even for those who have reached the place where heaven is a despairingly strained-toward afterlife, as a release and relief to the rigours and horrors of the here and now, a present day heaven would be a first choice if it weren't so unimaginable. This longed for, already tasted, sometimes-held-sometimes-lost rightness of life is the Kingdom of Heaven. When the Kingdom is experienced, we usually know it and appreciate it, even though we can't always define it or recognise its source. We know the feel of its breeze on our skin, naked and not ashamed.

Except there are also times when it disrupts, annoys and provokes in us reactions that seem the opposite of such peaceful satisfaction. Sometimes the presence of the Kingdom is experienced within and around us with an uncomfortable tension of glad rightness but also a secret and selfish bitter resentment, or even anger. It is so right and yet somehow feels aggravatingly wrong. We end up challenged to live differently, to think differently, to be different. One person's feeling of the ease of their own heavenly empire may lead to another's hell. The King's Kingdom may interrupt our own little fiefdom reveries with whiplash-creating collision. When something is wrong, and we want to be able to ignore it, a jolt from the Kingdom disturbs unjust false peace. This is usually an annoyingly awoken awareness rather than a soothingly irresponsible ignorance.

The fact that this Kingdom can be experienced by us with either joy or anger doesn't mean it is some kind of yin and yang thing, containing within itself both good and evil, peace and pain. This dichotomy is instead within us, because we not only have the image of the Kingdom imprinted into us, but we also have engrained other or opposing patterns that are often even more dominant. We groan with longing for the Kingdom and we groan with sickness against it, fighting it off as if it were some virus attacking our (unknowingly distorted) equilibrium. The apostle Paul writes that this kind of wrangle makes us wretched.[1] But that wretchedness doesn't necessarily inure us fully away from being God's image, although over time we do seem to become more used to the anti-Kingdom and its properties. For most of us, we still enjoy the delights of plan A, the song of the King. There's joy, peace, creativity

1. Romans 7:24.

and fulfilment to be had all around. It is not always easy to come by, and we are often robbed. We may even default to increasingly costly ways of purchasing it, or something like it, through money, power and appetites. But the free offer of the Kingdom of Heaven has been generously held in the open hand of God throughout every generation, for better for worse, for richer for poorer; in sickness and in health; close enough for every person to reach out, touch and receive.

I edit this introduction in the middle of the world's COVID 19 pandemic. This book has been in the making for the last decade or so, and therefore is definitely 'pre-covid'. Nevertheless, it is post-flood, post-exodus, post-exile, and post-resurrection. And in the light of the growth of the Kingdom of Jesus since his death and resurrection, it is also 'post' all number of horrific and wonderful experiences across cultures, places and times. I am sure that the current trembling and shaking across our world will emphasise certain aspects of this book and overshadow others, But the world is still "charged with the grandeur of God" and this Kingdom is on the increase.[2]

How to read this book

On the day of Pentecost when Peter was first touched with the new-making fire of the Holy Spirit, he spoke from the prophet Joel. Joel 2 is an incredible piece of poetic imagination. It describes this new, fiery, overflowing, flourishing age of the Spirit as one of dreaming and visioning. Peter, God-pointing the Pentecost crowds,

---

2. Hopkins, Gerard Manley, 1844-1889. "God's Grandeur" and Other Poems. New York: Dover Publications, 1995.

describes the gladness and joy of the disciples by saying "this is that".[3] "This", that you are seeing and experiencing, he says, "is that" which the prophet Joel was writing about. He is speaking about the Kingdom of Heaven, the central teaching of Jesus.

Reflecting on this message of Jesus, it appears that the Kingdom of Heaven is not just a new reality or world that we can aspire to, away from the pain and dysfunction of this one, nor is it confined to religious experience or the mission of the church. The Kingdom of Heaven, being experienced and lived out on this earth, was always God's plan for humanity and is also what the story and teaching of the Bible is about.

This is That explores some of the broad themes of the Kingdom of Heaven in five movements.

Part 1 outlines how the Kingdom plan is written into creation – into our humanity, our day to day, here and now. In spite of our falling, vandalising and self-harm, spectacularly written about across the books of the Bible, there is still an enjoying, yearning and relishing of the Kingdom of Heaven in our being and doing. This is the Genesis plan for humanity, to royally priest creation though the creative pressure of ruling and subduing, cultivating and keeping. It's what most of us do every day at work, at home or as we use our gifts and talents. But most of us don't know the anointing of the King as we live it out. Nevertheless, painted, hung or sprayed on cave, gallery and railway-arch walls is the story of our spreading towards a heavenly holy city that will one day reflect the glory of God and the beauty of his people.

---

3. Acts 2:16, KJV.

Part 2 explores the culture of the Kingdom, often described in the Bible as Shalom: the time and place where righteousness, peace and joy are experienced and celebrated. Shalom is a community where you don't just take a day off a week, but a year off every seven. Shalom is a deck chair, a market, a shared table, a harvest before we've ploughed their fields and scattered, an apple store of fruit, fashion, music, tech, health and joy. Shalom is also contested and fought over. Its growth should be natural, but so are the tumours of anti-Kingdom, empires of self-regard and self-fulfilment. These empires rise and fall, the toxic breathing of a sick creation. The goodness of God is undermined by the scheming of humanity's replicant machine version of family. But the response of God is not a bigger, better, bully-er kick of the jackboot. Instead, Shalom continues to be a family whose heartbeat rhythm of goodness and mercy spreads and gathers, further out, deeper in, breath by breath, inhaling promises and exhaling faith.

Part 3 is about Jesus and the good news message he proclaimed: the "gospel of the Kingdom".[4] According to the Bible, it is his life, teaching, death, resurrection and Spirit-breathing ascension that redeems and ignites afresh the Kingdom plan of heaven. He lived, acted and told stories and parables about it. Crucified as The King of the Jews, Jesus embodied the Kingdom of Heaven, and he did all this in a human body, with family, friends, enemies, stresses and strains weaving their own narratives in and out of his own experience. His stories show that the Kingdom of Heaven is as natural in creation as seeds, plants and harvests, and

4. Matthew 24:14.

13

that the Kingdom is most easily experienced as a feast, where there is always a place set for us. They also highlight the fact that this Kingdom is under attack because of its mustard seed power to spread its healing heat through the cold-hearted ranks of enemy opposition. Jesus tells it as a comedy that rewrites the tragedy of sickness and failure, and a drama that not only beats swords into ploughshares but also assertively and courageously declares full-out war on every power and principality, eventually through a lonely death outside the city and a quietly confident resurrection in morning garden.

Part 4 examines the roles of prophet, priest and king – biblical images and positions that shouldn't have to stay confined to Old Testament stories or church offices, but somehow describe how the Kingdom of Heaven is celebrated, governed and pointed towards by any person, in any place, at any time. God has designed his house and his household in such a way that its architecture fully reflects his reign. The garden, tabernacle, temple and church are actually great designs, filled with attractively creative patterns that don't have to remain in religion's realm but appeal to our love of form, organisation and relationship. And a case study of the prophet Elisha shows that it is more than possible to handle heaven and earth; joy and disappointment; success and failure; simplicity and power; as a regular human being in a culture that doesn't appear to really care one way or the other about the Kingdom of Heaven.

Part 5 is all about God-pointing – how to spot the signs of the Kingdom; what is new, or from a new age to come; what it means to suddenly really 'see', to say 'ah', to experience that old-fashioned word 'behold' in an exhilarating and delightful way. Jesus was a sign, pointing to a love that banishes our fears. He is the dramatist who holds a mirror up to nature, shows virtue her own feature, scorn her own image and the very age and body of the time his form and pressure – as Hamlet might say. He is the artist whose work connects who we are, what we do and where we live with who God is, what he does and where he lives. He is the bridegroom who connects fully in love and consummation, the beginning of a whole new Genesis family business.

Each of these five parts is split into smaller sections, most of which have a pause for reflection at the end. Like the Selah in a psalm, this is to allow for some space to lift up our eyes, look, and possibly behold a glimpse of the Kingdom not far from where we are. Some questions are given that may help give room for these moments.

Of course, the Kingdom of Heaven and its King are themes that the gospel writer, John, says are so huge that the world cannot contain the books that would try to describe them. This book is one of those human attempts to glimpse, sketch or brush against this most beautiful mystery – what it means to know that God lives among us; behold, Immanuel.

Part 1

The Genesis and Consummation of the Kingdom

In the beginning God created the heavens and the earth. [2] The earth was formless and void, and darkness was over the surface of the deep, and the Spirit of God was moving over the surface of the waters. [3] Then God said, "Let there be light"; and there was light. [4] God saw that the light was good; and God separated the light from the darkness. [5] God called the light day, and the darkness He called night. And there was evening and there was morning, one day.

[6] Then God said, "Let there be an expanse in the midst of the waters, and let it separate the waters from the waters." [7] God made the expanse, and separated the waters which were below the expanse from the waters which were above the expanse; and it was so. [8] God called the expanse heaven. And there was evening and there was morning, a second day.

[9] Then God said, "Let the waters below the heavens be gathered into one place, and let the dry land appear"; and it was so. [10] God called the dry land earth, and the gathering of the waters He called seas; and God saw that it was good. [11] Then God said, "Let the earth sprout vegetation, plants yielding seed, and fruit trees on the earth bearing fruit after their kind with seed in them"; and it was so. [12] The earth brought forth vegetation, plants yielding seed after their kind, and trees bearing fruit with seed in them, after their kind; and God saw that it was good. [13] There was evening and there was morning, a third day.

[14] Then God said, "Let there be lights in the expanse of the heavens to separate the day from the night, and let them be for signs and for seasons and for days and years; [15] and

let them be for lights in the expanse of the heavens to give light on the earth"; and it was so. ¹⁶ God made the two great lights, the greater light to govern the day, and the lesser light to govern the night; He made the stars also. ¹⁷ God placed them in the expanse of the heavens to give light on the earth, ¹⁸ and to govern the day and the night, and to separate the light from the darkness; and God saw that it was good. ¹⁹ There was evening and there was morning, a fourth day.

²⁰ Then God said, "Let the waters teem with swarms of living creatures, and let birds fly above the earth in the open expanse of the heavens." ²¹ God created the great sea monsters and every living creature that moves, with which the waters swarmed after their kind, and every winged bird after its kind; and God saw that it was good. ²² God blessed them, saying, "Be fruitful and multiply, and fill the waters in the seas, and let birds multiply on the earth." ²³ There was evening and there was morning, a fifth day.

²⁴ Then God said, "Let the earth bring forth living creatures after their kind: cattle and creeping things and beasts of the earth after their kind"; and it was so. ²⁵ God made the beasts of the earth after their kind, and the cattle after their kind, and everything that creeps on the ground after its kind; and God saw that it was good.

²⁶ Then God said, "Let Us make man in Our image, according to Our likeness; and let them rule over the fish of the sea and over the birds of the sky and over the cattle and over all the earth, and over every creeping thing that creeps on the earth." ²⁷ God created man in His own image, in the image of God He created him; male and female He created them.

[28] *God blessed them; and God said to them, "Be fruitful and multiply, and fill the earth, and subdue it; and rule over the fish of the sea and over the birds of the sky and over every living thing that moves on the earth."*

[29] *Then God said, "Behold, I have given you every plant yielding seed that is on the surface of all the earth, and every tree which has fruit yielding seed; it shall be food for you;* [30] *and to every beast of the earth and to every bird of the sky and to every thing that moves on the earth which has life, I have given every green plant for food"; and it was so.* [31] *God saw all that He had made, and behold, it was very good. And there was evening and there was morning, the sixth day.*

(Genesis 1)

Cake or Chaos

The Kingdom of Heaven is expressed in the message and life of Jesus. All his teaching, deeds and miracles seem to describe and embody the Kingdom. He talks about the Kingdom of Heaven a great deal and sums up his work and mission as proclaiming the arrival of its rule. This is not surprising if Jesus is the King of this Kingdom. Who, and where the King is, is what the Kingdom is like and where it is operating. Jesus' death and resurrection are the hinge on which the Kingdom of God turns, from being expressed in heaven (as well as deeply in the roots of creation) to a new earthly manifestation through the recapturing and reclaiming of a race that has been hauled into an enemy empire of slavery by a wicked dictator.

Jesus in Palestine is not the first century AD inventor of this new political/spiritual concept, though. Although this is clearly his message, he did not invent it as a timely new manifesto or as a special trademark for marketing his ideas into the next two millennia. (If that was his aim, however, he has done pretty well to introduce a brand that has infiltrated fashion, architecture, music, art, politics, healthcare, winter celebrations, candles and communion cups.) In fact, the idea of the Kingdom of Heaven runs through the whole of the story of God and his people. Its inception is found in the first two chapters and its climax in the last two chapters of the Bible.

Genesis 1 tells us that the creation of the world was energetic, busy, dramatic, colourful, imaginative, and totally extraordinary. What is fascinating is that the qualities and attributes revealed about God in His work are those that we each relish and delight in, too. It is as if He accomplished this project in a way that would utterly appeal to us in our God-imaged humanity: the ordering and separating and organising and completing; the chaos and action and impact and seeming lack of control once the ball is rolling. This is what we are like as makers, too. It is in this creative endeavour that we clearly see the rule of God, His Kingdom. He imagines it all, then does it all. And through it all, His reign has many fascinatingly familiar attributes.

Take, for example, "formless and void" in verse 2. The Spirit brooding, stirring, flapping and blowing over the watery stuff: what is that all about?[5] Some people point to the darkness, the writhing waters, the lack of form and emptiness (and the fact that it could be read as the earth 'became' like this rather than 'was' like this)[6] as evidence that the evil chaos of Satan's fall has already happened after verse 1, and God is now in the business of recreating a perfect world in the context of an opposing force, which would be an amazing act. God, in his purity and hope, recreating and ruling over forces that defy, and coming up with a newly beautiful planet and universe!

Alternatively, these two seemingly rather bleak words describing the primordial soup are simply describing a neutral chaos. A mess that is not morally wrong, but simply some substance that needs forming and filling; a challenge that God clearly rises to as he forms heavens and waters and earth in the first three days then fills them with stars

5. Genesis 1:2.
6. Reading this in such a way is linked to Gap Theory/Ruin-and-reconstruction Theory. More information can be found at: Custance, Arthur C. (2008). *Without Form and Void: A Study of the Meaning of Genesis 1:2* (reprint ed.). Classic Reprint Press.

and fish and birds and animals in the second three days. Isaiah 45 tells us that God's intention in his creation was not for the earth to be formless, but to be lived in.[7] So, assuming these waters are not the habitation of the previously fallen rebellious gods, then still they are waters ready for a bit of God-ordering and placing. They are waters that will separate and define what is above and what is below. And that is important because what is separated at this point may be intended to reconvene later in human and cosmic history. The darkness, then, is simply the state of the stuff that God has created, without his light energy yet to be spoken by his word.

Taking substance and making something of it: defining it, forming and fashioning it, filling it and then assessing its nature – these are activities that are inherently human, or inherently Godly and now imaged in humanity. Reigning over a place that is formless and void and giving it purpose is a Kingdom activity. A good king will identify a great place for a city, plan its construction and then invest. On a cosmic scale, this is what God the King did with the earth and heavens. On a smaller scale, this is what every human being does every day. And for a Brit in the Midlands, a great example of this is in the making of a chocolate cake. It is a domestic necessity to always have flour, eggs, butter, cocoa powder, and sugar to hand. Because within 30 minutes of wanting cake, you can be eating it! Sounds like the Kingdom to me.[8] The ingredients get flung into a bowl in a kind of chaos that is not only sin free but bursting with desire for the hands of the creator, or amateur baker, to form and fill. Or, in my case, to form and then be filled myself. The whisk

---

7. Isaiah 45:18.
8. Marie Antoinette's "Qu'ils mangent de la brioche" (let them eat cake) and the popular phrase "You can't have your cake and eat it" are just Kingdom counterfeits.

then hovers over the surface of the pudding and, as it gets put in a fiery oven, the metaphor ends up straying on to the pages of the book of Daniel, who sadly missed out on cake as a young man: we wake up and it's all a dream ...

How can we compare the first day of creation to making a cake? We can't and yet, because we are made in God's image, we find that his reigning over ingredients that he created and making something so beautiful as the earth is exactly what we each do – in tiny, even mundane ways – every day. The Kingdom of Heaven begins with the rule of God: declaring the truth, creating and making, separating and filling, judging and naming, making visible what is in his imagination, and then setting it free to generously reproduce within a reign of peace and rest. This looks like the activity of a human being, fully alive.

If this was fully and finally the Kingdom, then we know we would be safe and secure and very happy to continue in our flourishing. Nevertheless, there are other, equally inspiring aspects to the King's rule that are also embedded into these first actions of the cosmos.

Selah, pause, reflect

What activities do you enjoy that have a holy un-order about them?

When was the last time you played?

What is there in your heart that may look messy but is in fact truly good?

Kingdom creating always means doing it together

It is God the Father who is progenitor and King on these first pages of the Bible. It is his voice and his creating that speaks things into being. Yet the Christian God we come to know through the Bible is expressed as Father, Son and Holy Spirit. He is one God, and not one among many. The trinity embodies the fact that God is love, and so is in eternal relationship, expressing and knowing love within himself as Father and Son and Spirit. Trinity-lensed Christians see glimpses of this in Genesis 1, where God creates through his 'Word' – the description of Jesus the eternal Son, given by John – and the 'big wind' hovering could as easily be translated as 'Spirit of God'.[9] Then as God, singular, expresses the intention to create man, it is in "our image" and "our likeness" as plural.[10] Some denote this as a 'royal we', and some as a statement declared among the angelic beings already created. But as the man who is intended to be created also goes from singular 'man' to plural 'them', created in God's image, it certainly makes sense of the argument for Father, Son and Spirit speaking this together. This means that the first reigning of the Kingdom is not just done by an all-powerful dictator singularity. The decision comes from God the Father. The dictation is actually the person of Jesus, the Son, and the breath that forms those words and hovers over the

---

9. The 'Spirit of God' mentioned here, Ruach Elohim, can also be literally translated as Big Wind, and points towards the Day of Pentecost's pouring out of the Spirit and the noise of a violent wind that accompanied it.
10. Genesis 1:26.

first substance is the Spirit of God. Together they form and together they fill. Together God is reigning over the particles and the energy.

In the same way that we see the Son and Spirit on this page, so we see the Son in Proverbs 8, as Wisdom.[11] He exists, similar to the 'Word' described in John 1, with God and as God's Wisdom. He finds his source in the Father but has always been alongside the Father and his attitude at Creation is one of watching, working alongside, rejoicing and enjoying. The workshop of heaven was full of words, of breath. There were explosions of light and lots of water. It certainly wasn't a chaotic mess, but the imaginative energy and wild results must have been hilarious and exhilarating. Perhaps page one of the Bible was like a party game against the 6-day sand timer: Pictionary, playdough, building stuff with marshmallows and cocktail sticks. And when Adam joins in, no one can get the answers to the animal shapes because they haven't even got names yet, so they all end up giggling and laughing at each other's paper hats and party blowers.

The Kingdom of God, in the days of creation, is one of life-giving mutuality, even between those involved in the powerful act of creating. They are at each other's side, coworkers, deferring and honouring one another. As the story of God progresses, this becomes clearer and clearer, until finally the intention of God the Father is to give the Kingdom to King Jesus, his beloved Son, and because we find ourselves in Christ as His body, we also reign with Him. This is not simply a Kingdom of command and control, but

---

11. Proverbs 8:22-31.

of submission and delight with long-term goals to give things away very generously. In Genesis 1:26, even before people are created the intention is to give them the rule of the earth. *"Then God said, "Let Us make man in Our image, according to Our likeness; and let them rule over the fish of the sea and over the birds of the sky and over the cattle and over all the earth, and over every creeping thing that creeps on the earth."* Father, Son and Spirit all work together in ruling, and after only five and a half days they are planning to share this reign with a couple of naked hippies! The Kingdom of God is not so much about getting things done, as about enjoying doing these things together.

Selah, pause, reflect

Perichoresis is the term given to the dance within the Trinity; the constant interplay of giving away to one another.

If God's power and knowledge are an expression of this kind of love, what does this mean for our understanding of how God acts, and for our own human pursuit of power and knowledge?

"What's a heaven for?"

"In the beginning God created the heavens and the earth."[12]

How do we typically understand heaven?
Heaven is where God lives.
Heaven is where we want to live one day.
Angels and demons live in the heavens.
The heavens are the night-time skies, the galaxies and stars and planets.
The heavens are the skies where the birds live.

The word 'heavens' in Genesis 1 could have any of these meanings.

Verse 1 could be a title for the whole chapter.
As mentioned earlier, it could be an action that is spoiled or interfered with before Verse 2.
It could mean the creating of the earthly solid stuff as well as the skies we see just above us.
It could mean planet earth, its atmosphere and bio system, along with all the other worlds, stars and galaxies that stretch beyond.
It could be the creating of the physical and the natural worlds, as well as the spiritual and supernatural realms.

Because Genesis 1 is poetry, it can mean any and all these things at once. Poetry helps us to see and intuit concepts and experiences that are difficult to comprehend in a more linear or logical way. Love is better expressed in poetry

---

12. Genesis 1:1.

and song than as a series of equations, or descriptions of physical sensations and psychological triggers. Layers of meaning, drawing from multiple metaphors gained through experience and coupled with musicality and rhythm, is what language is all about. Poetry is often the language of worship. For some reason, we seem to best grasp truth and grace through crafted and passionate poetry. And by poetry, we may also mean the visual poetry of fine art, or the physical poetry of dance, or the aural poetry of music. The arts in culture are our way of expressing what we know, what we struggle with, what we aspire to.

It is no surprise, then, that the creation of heaven and earth is described not as scientific discourse but in poetry. There is a rhythm to the process we recognise as a week, within which are multiple rhythms of 'Then God said', or 'Let there be', or 'It was so', or 'It was good'.[13] There is movement, light and shade, colour and shape formed in our imagination as the chapter progresses. As we follow the words of Genesis 1, we begin to experience the majesty, ingenuity and creativity of the Creator King and feel our way towards a knowing – not a recipe or step by step guide to planet inventing – but who this King is, what he is like and why we have been created.

So, when we read the word 'heavens', the poetry of the word of God unlocks for us the beginning of an exploration and journey of discovery that is embedded in the heart of God's Kingdom plan. The heavens are indeed the place where the planets and stars are. And when we look up at night, most of us are filled with awe and longing and

---

13. Gen 1:3-4 and throughout.

amazement. We feel small in comparison, and yet hugely personally significant, possibly because we do have such a self-aware ability to see how small we are. Many cultures equate the stars and planets with their Gods. Even in our own increasingly rational setting, the exploration of matter in and beyond our galaxy is all consuming. Outer space, how it is formed and what else might be there, represents for us the unattainable, or the attainable if we stretch a bit further. It is within reach and yet when we stretch out our hands, we cannot fully touch it. "A man's reach should exceed his grasp, or what's a heaven for?"[14]

So, the heavens that are filled on day 4 and day 5, with lights and birds, are our physical outer space, and inner atmosphere, night and day skies. They can also be those spiritual heavenly places, filled with angels and heaven borne beings. And we know that these beings were singing and shouting for joy during the making of God's earth.[15] We have words and metaphors that are mingling our experience of the physical with our yearning for the spiritual. Heaven and earth are separated from one another and yet close enough to touch. In fact, it is very hard to determine where the sky actually starts. Is it where the birds are, or above even that? When you travel in a plane, you are travelling in the sky. At what point is the plane not in the sky? When it touches the runway, or 6 feet above it? The Everest climber is as firmly rooted as you and I standing on a commuter platform, and yet they feel on the edge of eternity. The unattainable heavens can be seen from the earth, and yet somehow begin wherever they touch the earth. In the

---

14. Browning, Robert. "Andrea del Sarto." First published in 1855, found in full here: https://www.poetryfoundation.org/poems/43745/andrea-del-sarto.
15. Job 38:7.

same way, the Kingdom of the heavens, where God lives, or where his angels exist, is way beyond us, visible in our imagination, but beyond our grasp. And yet, like the sky, it is surrounding us, breezing upon us, filling our lungs, and close enough to jump up into and around.

Inbuilt into these days of creating are cosmic beings that cause us to wonder, and beautiful birds that cause us to long to fly. There is awareness that there is more to life than that which we can simply see and touch. But this 'more' is not necessarily some better or other world that was created first as a superior template. Instead it touches and surrounds and fills the earth that we find ourselves on. The Kingdom of Heaven is all around in Genesis 1, wooing us and fascinating us towards the Creator. It is the air we breathe and the biosphere that sustains us. It is already our home, and as the story of God progresses, our multiplication and fruitfulness and deepening of relationship with the King will invite this Kingdom to full-fill His creation.

Selah, pause, reflect

Look at the sky for a few minutes. Slow down. Experience the vastness of everything that has been created.

Watch the effect of the wind – on the trees, grass, washing on a line, a flag. Think about this.

"I say to you, unless one is born of water and the Spirit he cannot enter into the Kingdom of God. That which is born of the flesh is flesh, and that which is born of the Spirit is spirit. Do not be amazed that I said to you, 'You must be born again.' The wind blows where it wishes and you hear the sound of it, but do not know where it comes from and where it is going; so is everyone who is born of the Spirit."[16]

16. John 3:5-8.

What I do is me: for that I came

The culture of this new heavens and earth Kingdom in Genesis 1 is one where there is plenty of order and ruling and decision making and governing. Nevertheless, this is done in joyful relationship, with new-daily creativity and then millions of years of freedom to explore what it is 'to be'.

As each creation day progresses there are more ideas being spoken out, and the phrases that are used are 'Let there be', or 'let the' or 'let them'.[17] We are so used to this creation command that we forget that it doesn't sound so much like a command that should be obeyed, but rather as a flung wide-open door to opportunities and characteristics that are ready to burst out with energy. To let something be or do is to give it permission, to give freedom, to allow, to recognise what is inherent and unlock potential. When we say 'Let the games begin!' it is not usually a command for people to quickly put on their shorts and vests and run whatever sack or egg and spoon race we tell them to. They are already there, dressed, prepared, jostling for position on the line, revving their engines for the chequered flag to finally go down. Rather than God saying the waters must do this, or the earth must do that, he speaks the word, then, figuratively speaking, steps back and gives room for that word to energise and inhabit and give life to whatever is being created or made. This is a fascinating way of setting up a new Kingdom. It is not anarchic – there is the poetic order and strong direction that makes it all happen. But neither

---

17. Gen 1:3 and throughout.

is it despotic and machine-like. The species have their own kind, but are released to reproduce, to even multiply and fill the earth, with no written constitution, memorandum and articles, caveats or CCTV. There is plenty of teeming and swarming – millions of excited new creatures on their way to the beach or the mountains or just hanging out with mates. And the voice of God is calm and strong, speaking encouragement to the seeds of new life and their natural taxonomic processes.

The initial spurt of life energy in the act of creation has generous permission as its source and then an anticipation of free abundance and continued creativity as its expectation. It is not a casual take it or leave it suggestion to be fruitful, to multiply and to fill, to be what or who you really are and to perhaps be it well: it is a command of the King. Even though God is the only one who could have done any of the work in those creation days, his eye is not on himself but on the life to be enjoyed by the creatures he has made. God knows what makes creatures the beings they really are – whether that's a kingfisher or a dragonfly – and his intention is that they fulfil this destiny, individually and as a part of the whole heaven and earth Kingdom.

God knows that the sun is great at giving light and generally holding stuff together for the galaxy. God knows too what makes spiritual authorities and rulers tick. They love to govern. So, the Sun and Moon, as physical entities or as representatives of spiritual beings, are given the task of governing. And mankind: what do men and women like doing? The act (and the consequence) of making more men and women. So God says be fruitful. People also love to do stuff and make things – we are in God's image after all – so

God says, "Fill the earth."[18] We love to take something and explore it, or extend it, or play with it, or add to it. So God says, "Multiply."[19] And people love to organise, and lead and influence and work, so God says in Verse 16, when he's considering the human project, "Let them rule." And when they have been created, he commands them to subdue the earth and rule over the creatures, which probably includes playing and cooking and singing and driving and setting fire to things.[20] It is a perfect Kingly command because it suits us so well. And we are told to do it in abundance, as much as we like! God's reign in Genesis 1 is the most exciting, demanding, challenging and joyful dominion a person, snail, halibut, daffodil or pebble could ever imagine being a part of.

This Kingdom of creatures and people set free to be who they are and to do what they do is wonderfully imagined by Gerard Manley Hopkins in his poem 'As Kingfishers Catch Fire'.[21]

AS kingfishers catch fire, dragonflies dráw fláme;
As tumbled over rim in roundy wells
Stones ring; like each tucked string tells, each hung bell's
Bow swung finds tongue to fling out broad its name;
Each mortal thing does one thing and the same:
Deals out that being indoors each one dwells;
Selves—goes itself; myself it speaks and spells,
Crying Whát I do is me: for that I came.
Í say móre: the just man justices;

18. Genesis 1:28.
19. Genesis 1:28
20. Genesis 1:28.
21. Hopkins, Gerard Manley. "As Kingfishers catch Fire." Found in *Gerard Manley Hopkins: Poems and Prose*, Penguin Classics, 1985.

Kéeps gráce: thát keeps all his goings graces;
Acts in God's eye what in God's eye he is
Chríst—for Christ plays in ten thousand places,
Lovely in limbs, and lovely in eyes not his
To the Father through the features of men's faces.

This is the kind of Kingdom that God the Creator designed: one of freedom, exultation and a natural overflow of praise. Hopkins calls this sense of self-identity, Inscape. It is the inherent quality and projection of a creature. Theologians Duns Scotus and Thomas Merton might call it "Thingness".[22] I call it "Ishness". You are very (insert your name here)-ish! To be who you are and to be it well is what God's generous Kingdom is all about. Simply using a skill can give us incredible satisfaction. Or lying on a Mediterranean beach may be where you feel most yourself! (In which case, we should certainly ask ourselves whether God wants us to do more of this kind of devotion and worship!) Moments in a relationship, walking in a particular place, engaging with and accomplishing a task: there are experiences of pleasure or perhaps determination where we know a profound significance. Some religions are attempts to find and sustain this through emptying or filling, quite often to the exclusion of all else. But it is best expressed in harmony with the Creator and his creation. He is very keen that every plant and every creature expresses its 'ishness' in such a way that it gives of itself and multiplies itself. This is what praise is at its best and most real. And at the heart of this praising, singing, expressing Kingdom is Christ – the king, the model, the centrepiece, cornerstone and capstone.

---

22. Hialmarson, Leonard E. An Emerging Dictionary for the Gospel and Culture: A Conversation from Augustine to Zizek. Oregon: Wipf and Stock, 2010.

Selah, pause, reflect

My friend Ethan, a filmmaker in Birmingham USA, told me that he spent a month's vacation making furniture. He had been paid for a previous media job with some credit for a hardwood store so had access to all the material he wanted. As he worked, he listened to an audiobook of *Creativity, Inc.*, written by Pixar founder Ed Catmull, and then another, a biography of the designer Sir Jony Ive by Leaner Kahney. These reflections on creativity filled his soul as he made. And he found that with garage door opened, a clear blue sky and plenty of sunlight, he worked hard without perspiration. This was not toil by the sweat of his brow. Ethan writes:

> It was 30 straight days of vacation, everyday in the shop taking a break from filmmaking and making several furniture pieces. It was the most inspiring and worshipful time I've had in a very long while . . . listening to the book on Mr. Ive which is all about design while I'm constantly making design choices . . . Ahhh! I wish I was back there doing that again.

This was who Ethan was created to be. He fully lived out his sense of 'called' self – physically, emotionally, mentally and spiritually. "What he does is him; for that he came."[23] The Kingdom of Heaven is at hand, in a garage on a bright winter's day.

---

23. Ibid.

The King's Speech – to rule and subdue

Some of the most significant language in these creation chapters is language of governance. On day 4, when we have the insight into heavenly places that are both physically and spiritually cosmic, the two great lights are given the purpose of ruling or governing. Since the growth and activity of creation is maintained and measured by time, then the ruling of the sun and moon is our constant. If the sun, the moon, and the stars alongside them are also representatives of spiritual realities and beings, then we also have our first glimpse of an order and rule that is spiritually heavenly. There is an order above which is reflected by the new order to be established and then maintained by humanity below. There are increasing glimpses into the rule that is happening in the unseen realms as the Bible story progresses. Most often these glimpses reveal where that rule is broken, or corrupted. There are moments when the governing in heavenly realms clearly affects what is happening in the earthly domains, such as Genesis 6 and the book of Job; in the ministry of Jesus we clearly see how the good rule of man on the earth affects what is happening in heavenly places.[24]

It seems that there is order in the creation of the world. There is a reign whose authority puts things in their proper places, which in turn then leads to a freedom to multiply and fill without the need for many more strict commands. The two great lights have dominion over the earth in

---

24. Genesis 6:1-5, Job 1.

verse 16 and 18 of Genesis 1, described in a similar way to the dominion of Solomon and Hezekiah who ruled over households and peoples later in the story of Israel.[25] The sun and moon don't seem to lose their tempers – their governing is not cruel or selfish. They are more like the governesses Mary Poppins or Nanny McPhee: full of surprises but with a constancy that is incredibly secure. It is God who has set everything in its place, who then delegates ruling authority to the heavenly lights. So, it is no surprise that he then uses more Kingdom language of ruling and reigning when commissioning mankind.

In verse 26, the plan of the Father, with the Son and Spirit, is that people made in his image will rule over the creatures of the earth. In verse 28, these newly created ones are told specifically to subdue the earth and rule over its creatures, alongside being fruitful, multiplying and filling the place: "God blessed them; and God said to them, 'Be fruitful and multiply, and fill the earth, and subdue it; and rule over the fish of the sea and over the birds of the sky and over every living thing that moves on the earth.'"[26] Then God said, "Let Us make man in Our image, according to Our likeness."[27] To be made in the image and likeness of God the Father, Son and Spirit tells us about who we are and how we may function.

Whether there is an intended difference between image and likeness, to do with moral attributes or spiritual life, or if the two words are simply defining one another through their poetry, human beings are meant to rule like

---

25. 1 Kings 9:19, 2 Kings 20:13. See also Psalm 145:13 for God's governing of His everlasting Kingdom
26. Genesis 1:28.
27. Genesis 1:26.

God. To hold the image of the ruler, whether on a coin as legitimate currency; or the imprint of a ring; the signature of the president; the swipe card of the corporation; or even the retina pattern of the King's own eyes, we then have authority to speak and wield power. And because the Bible tells us that human beings are the apple of God's eye, then not only can we see ourselves best mirrored in his pupils, but the closer we are to him, the more we really do reflect the King's own retina pattern.[28]

To be God's likeness on the earth is to be licensed to rule as his representative. To be in God's image is to have the same qualities to be able to rule in the same way as the King. As Hamlet said of his father, the king, "a combination and a form indeed/ Where every god did seem to set his seal/ to give the world assurance of a man".[29] Reigning is an inbuilt, natural human function that begins with our joyful handling of materials, plants, creatures and one another in furthering the earth-filling plan of God.

To subdue somewhere, something or even someone is a strong action. It is the same word used in the Bible when people have been forcibly oppressed. There are also implications of treading in the word used here.[30] It is a word used when Israel took the promised land in Joshua and Numbers – not surprisingly, as Joshua is told earlier that taking the land will be done by each footstep he takes.[31] This is sung about in Psalm 8, where the creatures of the heavens and earth are celebrated for the glory they bring to God, and mankind shares this celebration because

28. Psalm 17:8, Zechariah 2:8.
29. Hamlet: Act 3, Scene 4.
30. Micah 7:19.
31. Joshua 18:1, Numbers 32:22-29.

of the honour he is given in having the creatures of the earth sit under his feet.[32] Given the joy and freedom of the earth in its command to yield its fruit, it is unlikely that God is now commissioning mankind to subjugate it like a slave. Unfortunately, after thousands of years of slavery and oppression, there will be many groups that read this word on the first page of the Bible and automatically then see it as evidence of God's and man's cruelty; in fact, a command to be brutal. Therefore, we may need to reframe our understanding of the word subdue, unhooking it from a purely aggressive meaning and attaching it to the assertiveness of love and kindness.

Nevertheless, the force of the word is really important. To get the best out of anything, there needs to be a certain amount of (loving) creative pressure, a subduing and a treading down. To use a somewhat biblical image, grapes are trodden in order to release their juice to make wine to make people glad. A grape is not coaxed into releasing its juice by a lullaby or stroking its skin. A baby, however, is subdued by stroking its skin and singing a lullaby, but not usually by being trodden upon.[33] Subduing is therefore creative pressure that is applied appropriately to make, form or fashion. You might say Genesis 2 sees God subduing the dust in order to make Adam and subduing the side of man in order to fashion Eve.

We are subduing all the time and thoroughly enjoying its challenge. Making a cup of tea demands the subduing of water, the subduing of tea leaves, the subduing of a cow's

---

32. Psalm 8:6. Ruling and 'under foot' are mentioned together
33. Observe artist Jonathas de Andrade's film "O Piexe" for a sinister caressing subduing which highlights the continuing subtle subjugation of people and race.

udder. The pressure of an artist's pencil on paper subdues these materials to the letting be of an artistic idea. A kiss (performed properly) demands a slight pursing of the lips, followed by a slight pressing onto another's pursed lips. Without any creative pressure here, the kiss ends up limp and flaccid. (Try a non-subdued kissing action next time you are feeling romantic and watch the results – dribble and a slap round the face.)

Mankind is also commissioned to rule over the creatures. Again, there is a certain pressure that may be applied in such ruling, but good governance has clearly defined boundaries, areas of resistance that can be used to build strength and encourage ingenuity. Rules lead to creativity – the structure of a sonnet or a tweet forces the artist to dig deeper. Rules encourage sports men and women to work out new ways to train and new skills to hone in order to win. The rules I broke when playing Monopoly against my brother by hiding money when he went to the loo didn't increase my pleasure of the game and never led to me winning. Conversely, he can play a game he's never known before and suddenly know it better than anyone, imposing new rules I hadn't ever experienced before. (There's clearly still some unresolved competition in this relationship . . .) Ruling is an awesome responsibility. For a new parent to rule over a newborn baby – feeding, changing, caring and nurturing – is terrifying. Where do we start in those first hours once the midwife has gone? The child needs our rule – hands on, up close and personal – flowing from a heart that bursts with new-found love.

This ruling and subduing is how mankind will affect the growing and filling, spoken by God to the earth and its creatures, in such a way that it brings glory to God and a flourishing to the earth's inhabitants. This Kingdom rule of God is going to spread throughout creation as it fills and multiplies, through the delegated authority and power given to people. Because people are made in God's image, it is the most natural thing for them to subdue and to rule in a similar way to God. (They may not 'create' in quite the same way. Creating in that way of something-out-of-seeming-nothing, out of Godself and his creative word-imagination, is only in the realm of the Godhead.) Imagining and designing and making and building is something that people do. In fact, we can't help but do it. Every time we do, we are fulfilling these first commands of the Kingdom of God. Which is why, according to Hopkins' poem earlier, our being and doing is so transcendent and spiritually fulfilling. The purpose of God is that creation is filled with his rule, through people, which is an act of worship and an intimate invitation to God to live among us and enjoyably judge our endeavours.

The first steps for Adam and Eve in inhabiting, inviting and extending the Kingdom of God were simply in obeying those commands to subdue and rule. For us, with such a broken and confused earth, it is now harder to subdue and rule without breaking, corrupting or abusing the earth, creatures and people we are exercising our influence among. But the imprint of God has not been wiped from us, and the grace of God proves that all over the world, human beings are still enjoying fulfilling the first Kingdom mandate. The connection to the materials they are working with, the fruit of their labour, the nature of coworking: all these are deeply fulfilling, bringing satisfaction and rest, and continuing to delight God the creator King.

Selah, pause, reflect

Take a few minutes to rule and subdue now. Make a drink; tidy up; write something down; cut the lawn.

What does it feel like to engage in the first commission given to humanity?

Can you do this with joy and without compulsion?

In what way is the earth, the stuff, and those around, now better off because you have joined in the rule of the Kingdom of Heaven in this way?

Protect and Serve;
Form and Fashion

Genesis 2 locates the earth-filling Kingdom plan firmly in a place. Once again, God is instigating and considering, making and fashioning, and, like any good artist-ruler, defining and refining his work in progress.

The language used in this chapter regarding man's responsibility relates to his role as gardener and steward of the earth's resources. This does not clash with Genesis 1's vocabulary of governing but reveals that the creative pressure of subduing and ruling is in order to bring out the best and guard against the worst. Man is placed in the garden in order to cultivate and keep it. Elsewhere in the Bible, the word 'cultivate' means to serve,[34] and is even used of the serving of God as our act of worship.[35] When we cultivate, or till the ground, we serve it in such a way that it can be fruitful. We tend to it, meeting its needs so that it may flourish. Our worship of God in this way does not somehow improve him, or make him a better God, but makes room for his truth and grace in to flourish in our lives and on the earth. This image also shows that our subduing in no way undermines the command to cultivate and serve the earth. A garden is a wonderful example of this. A garden is a place of interaction between people and nature. Designed for men and women's delight, it is also for the delight of the plants and animals that live there. Their

---

34. Exodus 8-10.
35. Exodus 3:12.

glory is displayed and beauty is revealed. They are fed and watered and given space to grow. The wonderfully messy jungle of day 3 and day 6 is already good, but when God and then man get their hands on it, then it can more self-consciously shout, in Hopkins' words, "What I do is me, for that I came".[36]

Most of us look out at our gardens in March and have an urge to cultivate. For some reason, gardens get filled with plastic bags, brushless broom handles, broken buckets and deflated footballs. We long to serve this blessed plot and turn it into a paradise, with delicately urinating cherubs or splashes of untamed colour. The spirit may be willing but the flesh is often weak. But in most people, hope rises when they see a well-cultivated garden. The word cultivate is also used to simply mean 'work'. Work is good. It is not a curse but an inbuilt motivation where we cannot help but cultivate, get our hands dirty, use some force, make something happen. Because work is so often linked to our survival or experience of oppression, serving has become a forced-upon duty rather than an inevitable joy. But cultivating, serving and working are actually some of the glories of being human.

The word to 'keep' is to protect or to guard. It is about being watchful, paying attention, being vigilant.[37] We talk today about people who 'keep' certain plants, or animals. They look after them, probably rather obsessively, because they are fascinated, interested and full of care towards them. The words cultivate and keep show us the attitude

---

36. Hopkins, Gerard Manley. "As Kingfishers catch Fire." Found in *Gerard Manley Hopkins: Poems and Prose*, Penguin Classics, 1985
37. Deuteronomy 2:4, Nehemiah 11:19.

of compassion and justice that are in the heart of God, and the importance of detail within the broad sweep of reigning over creation. They are the motivations for how we use our skills and gifts in the ruling and subduing that we cannot help but do. They are words that imply soft hearts and keen minds, but they are no less words of the Kingdom than subduing and ruling. In fact, we see synonyms of cultivate and keep within slogans of police forces round the world today. In 1955, LAPD chose 'To Protect and Serve' as their motto, an aspiration to be good and not harsh rulers.

The nature of our rule is well demonstrated in the fun process through which God takes Adam to find a suitable partner.[38] There are of course some difficulties if this is read as a simple continuation of narrative from Genesis 1, as the animals seem already to have been made in that account. Some describe this making as the creating of a few garden animals, or it could be read, as in the NIV, that the Lord had already made these animals.[39] What is exciting about this episode is God's insight regarding Adam's personal state and then His idea to do something to refine it. Rather than doing the naming or calling of the creatures himself, He steps back and lets the man do this, giving to Adam the implied authority that comes with naming. And then God sees what Adam will call them! God is interested in watching and finding out. It is not that God is clueless or helplessly at Adam's crazy-naming mercy, but there is a partnering in the reign happening here. God is truly interested in how we go about exercising our rule and implementing our image-of-God nature. It seems possible here for us to genuinely delight God in the work we do. God

38. Genesis 2:18-20.
39. Genesis 2:19.

is watching to see what names Adam gives to the animals. This corresponds to his observing how we respond to new discoveries, how we define and categorise these findings. Perhaps also in view here is the 'how' of Adam's 'calling' of the creatures; his speaking and communicating, the rapport he develops with the creatures. In the same way, we may consider God observing how we invent vocabulary, how we then communicate and use media and signs and sounds.

Each new discovery of ours is not necessarily a surprise to God, but our reign clearly fascinates him. He must enjoy our enjoyment, and perhaps as a Father after all, he is in some way actually surprised and gladdened by our responses and methods and conclusions. This means that he delights in and is honoured by our inquisitive stewarding, our scientific exploration, and our ceaseless fascination with language, words and images. The intimacy between God and mankind in Genesis 2 gives an insight that He is genuinely in relationship with people. It is not simply anthropomorphic to think of God as being delighted in people, any more than his walking around the garden is a demeaning and crass description of the behaviour of the creator of the universe. He really is beyond our imaginings: that He can both create everything and then also enjoy it can confuse us. Is he all powerful and therefore too big to be influenced by creation? Or is he so at the mercy of what is happening around Him that he has no self-determination? Genesis 1 and 2 demonstrate both: that he holds all power and he also loves passionately and fully. He really is unpindownable and not like any God we have invented.

Selah, pause, reflect

David Young was an electrical engineer. He was husband to Joy and father to three children, including myself. He was a committed follower of Jesus and has served faithfully in church all his life, variously as a deacon, elder, secretary and treasurer.. How might he understand his reigning with Jesus in the Kingdom?

Obviously, serving in church seems to be a traditionally straightforward and understandable way that a Christian like my dad would engage in the Kingdom. In fact for 50 years he welcomed people on the door, young and old alike, helping to establish a culture of kindness and embrace. We would also see his faithfulness as a husband, exemplary and wonderful to witness especially over the fifteen years that my mother lived with Alzheimer's. Dad proved his devotion and commitment to Joy until she sadly died, as well as being a great father in bringing up the three of us. Being fruitful and faithful in these relationships is central to the way that God wants us to rule with Him. So, what about his 40 plus years of working as an electrical engineer? Was this simply a way of him fulfilling his function of looking after his family, or giving to generously to church funds? It is not what we do, of course, but how we do it that reveals our character and builds treasure. But how much does electrical engineering fit with the Kingdom of God? Are certain jobs more or less Kingdom oriented?

Dad specialism was in a branch of electrical engineering known as FACTS – Flexible AC Transmission Systems.

He was instrumental in designing the Static Var Compensator. Yes, one of those! It's all to do with power and current and whether or not there's too much or not enough. When there's a load of power being sent to something that fluctuates in its demand, then there can end up being too much or not enough flow. This is similar to too many people having a shower in the same house at once: annoyingly too hot or cold, dribbling then gushing. With electricity, this results in lights flickering and other items not working properly. A Static Var Compensator responds quickly to smooth out the fluctuations by providing some reactive power that will stop the whole thing being too inductive or capacitive, too high or low. Rather than blowing up the town, or dribbling in an occasional bit of electricity, the SVC makes sure we're all OK for hairdryers, microwaves and Xboxes.

Basically, power needs plenty of subduing. Electricity is great, but you don't want to keep too much of it in your pocket or by the back door. But when it is subdued, it is safe to use and amazing! Dad has put SCVs into CERN in Switzerland to make sure the Large Hadron Collider doesn't blow up, into Ethiopia where the supply of electricity is not always consistent, into factories in Sheffield and at the end of long runs of transmission in the Australian outback.

Clearly I haven't a clue what any of this is about, but all those technical words sound good. "What I do is me, for that I came" shouts the SVC, the electrical engineer, the arc furnace, the electric guitarist.[40] What dad had

---

40. Hopkins, Gerard Manley. "As Kingfishers catch Fire." Found in *Gerard Manley Hopkins: Poems and Prose*, Penguin Classics, 1985.

done, with his mentor and friend Dr Erich Freidlander who came up with the idea in the 1930s, was to successfully subdue the earth, with plenty of creativity, scientific theory and hands on creative pressure. This problem to be solved must have been somewhere in God's massive mind, millions of years ago. Because God knew that sending power a long way would be tricky, he brought the problem to David and Erich, like his including of Adam in the garden project, to see how they would name and make their solution. And I think he saw that it was good.

Sadly, my father died after a short and serious illness just a few months before this book was published. He himself had just written a contribution to an international technical manual on Flexible AC Transmission Systems. What struck me during his illness and after his death were the heartfelt tributes of his colleagues from around the world, 20 years after his retirement, all lauding him as a truly 'Great Engineer'; and someone with integrity, a delight in finding solutions and getting things absolutely right, and an inspiration for others to continue to enjoyably excel. This is That, which the prophets spoke about, character, skill, wisdom and love, in the poetry of Proverbs 8:30,31.

Then I was beside Him, as a master workman;
And I was daily His delight,
Rejoicing always before Him,
Rejoicing in the world, His earth,
And having my delight in the sons of men.

Servant Leaders

Psalm 24 says: *The earth is the LORD'S, and all it contains.*

Psalm 115 says: *The earth He has given to the sons of men.*

The earth still belongs to God, and He is its ultimate ruler. He continues to rule from heaven, and Psalm 115 also says that "the Heavens are the heavens of the Lord". This Psalm is affirming that God has delegated His kingly authority to rule to people. There is a difference between being an owner or being a steward. Jesus often uses parables to describe God as an owner and people as His stewards. Hopefully the same kind of rule happens through the stewards as through the King of Kings, but it is the King who is ultimately in charge and not the stewards.

Genesis 2 makes this clear in the positioning of the garden, the trees and mankind. In chapter 1, mankind is clearly the pinnacle of creation, male and female were 'very good'. In chapter 2, we see what becomes central. Man is made and Eden is where God plants his garden. Man is put in the garden and told to look after it. Man is brought from the outside in. The garden was not planted and built around him so he could lord it over the place. Neither was the garden, planted to the east of Eden, central to everything, and mankind only there to worship it. Instead, it is the tree of life that is central.[41] The more we read the Bible, the more we see that the tree of life represents the source of

---

41. Genesis 2:9.

life in God and more specifically the person of Jesus, who said that he was Life; satisfying hunger and thirst as people feed on Him.

The tree of the knowledge of good and evil is mentioned at the same time as the tree of life, but not specifically as central. Eve, however, in her confusion and panic over the serpent's manipulation, mentions it being in the middle of the garden.[42] This tree is not about enabling humanity in being wise rulers, whose fruit would only benefit Adam and Eve. Instead, it is the temptation to be central, to be in the place where all judgements are measured from. To judge what is good and evil according to what we think. This is the difference between being the owner king and being the servant rulers. In Christ, the tree of life, God is at the centre of this new garden project. He is creator and therefore has the wise judgement on all things. As co-regents, we rule with Him and because He is so accessible, we can consult, learn and feed off him any time we like help in the task of protecting and serving. Our rule gets corrupted when we deny the fact that we have been brought from the dust of the margins into this beautiful paradise, and instead we assume the King's prerogative as owner. Because we are creatures and not the Creator, this means that we become judgemental – not the same as having the ability to judge. We become religious in spirit and not simply able to enjoy the love of the presence of God. We subdue and rule with oppression because we arrogantly feel we know what is right and wrong.

The Kingdom project works so well because of the grace and truth of God. His grace invites us to enjoy the whole of

---

42. Genesis 3:3.

creation and get our hands on it as rulers. His truth means that we are not asked, as a collection of dust particles, to imperiously judge another collection of dust particles. He has the perspective, reigning from the heaven of heavens, and can see not only the physical, as we can, and the psychological, as we have also learned to at times, but He can see the spiritual. In those first days in Eden, it looks like there was a regular appointment that God kept with Adam and Eve at the end of each day.[43] Perhaps this was to share experiences, ask questions, show and tell, drink wine and each cheese and olives, listen to music or watch a film. Clearly this time of connection was very important for God and for Adam and Eve. Strolling and chatting, arm in arm – this is what friends, lovers, and children with their parents do. God is God, King of Kings. Man is man, servant king of the garden. Ruling and reigning together requires some reflection, dialogue and sharing of ideas. At the end of Genesis 2 it is all very good, and the plan is to let it grow.

Selah, pause, reflect

Is it serving or ruling that most threatens you?

In what areas of ruling do you feel the privilege of serving? And what aspect of service demands the most ruling from you?

Which leader inspires you most with their character of servant king?

---

43. Genesis 3:8-10.

Extending the garden and filling the earth

The command to multiply, be fruitful and fill the earth is a daunting one, given a planet our size and a couple of newly formed human beings who don't have a car or the means to make a refreshing cup of tea after work. So it is God's grace that gets the project off to a start, by making an example of what can be. The garden is made by God for the man and woman to live and work in. This is a paradise, a walled garden, which is designed and executed as a home and inspirational template to extend, replicate and complete. Middle Eastern gardens typically are designed with light and shade, irrigation systems of pools and channels of water, lush trees and fruits and preferably large trays of Mediterranean honey, nut and butter soaked pastries.

So, what may have been the reason for this garden plan? Somehow, the earth needed people to exercise dominion over it and the garden was the example of how to do this. The Kingdom of God was to extend from this place to cover the earth and Adam and Eve were the first ones to exercise this authority. The result, over time, would be a garden that was also full of dwellings, to house all the people that would eventually come along. To make this possible, Adam and Eve would have to get to know one another more fully, and get to know the planet, its materials and properties. They would then have to work out how to build a family beyond a number where they knew everyone by name; a community with a culture of the love, freedom and rule of

God at its heart. They would also have to get to know God more, as would all their offspring. By Genesis 3, Adam and Eve are working the garden and knowing God's presence in a specific place at a specific time. We know from the rest of the Bible that the desire of God is for his presence to fill everything in every way. Surely his plan was to allow Adam and Eve to discover more of his love and be filled with his breath, then to do their reigning, cultivating work in the joy of this, transmitting what they discovered in God to everything they touched.

The garden has the beginnings of everything Adam and Eve need for God's huge construction project. The tree of life is at the centre, their source of grace and peace. The tree of the knowledge of good and evil is there as a reminder of the truth of who they are, making it possible for them to choose his Kingship in their lives out of love, rather than having no option but to submit. They have food from all the trees and water from the river. The river that flows into the garden to water it comes simply 'out of Eden'. There always seems to be a river that God provides, whether it is from a rock, from the Temple, from His throne, from Jesus or from the innermost being of the believer. This Eden river then divides into four heads. In the Septuagint, not surprisingly bearing in mind the overarching Kingdom theme, this is the same word used elsewhere for the beginning, the first placed and the ruler. The four rivers have their source and rule in the garden, probably then flowing in the four directions of the compass, to water the whole earth.

Whatever has its beginning in the garden, then follows the flow of the river. As the garden is watered, so it then has the capacity to extend out and beyond. As the garden is tended, then the land beyond the garden can also be developed and served in a similar way. If the garden is good for the people, animals and plants whose habitat it is, then why limit it? Why not generously extend all that is good to the four corners of the earth?

The first river, Pishon, is said to flow round the land of Havilah, where there is gold, bdellium (a pearl like, perfumed resin) and onyx stone. Follow the river and you will find precious minerals, metals and stones. Follow it through the Bible and these stones are built into the priests' clothing and into the new city. Follow it to Qatar and there's oil. Follow it as far as Normandy in France and you'll find precious smelly Camembert. Follow it to both Birminghams, UK and USA, and there's iron ore, limestone and coal. Follow it to Peru, and there are anchovies. (I only know this because 'And anchovies from Peru' was the first line I ever learned and performed, age 5, in the school assembly.) As the garden extends, so too will Adam and Eve and their growing family find the resources they need to carry on gardening and building. This is a Kingdom activity: to navigate and explore.

Proverbs 25:2 says:

> It is the glory of God to conceal a matter,
> But the glory of kings is to search out a matter.

God has hidden away such riches in the earth for mankind to discover. The first naming of the animals must have shown Adam that there was a long way to go in learning about God's earth. But this appetite for learning is the glory of a king.

The proverbs continue:

> *³ As the heavens for height and the earth for depth,*
> *So the heart of kings is unsearchable.*
> *⁴ Take away the dross from the silver,*
> *And there comes out a vessel for the smith;*
> *⁵ Take away the wicked before the king,*
> *And his throne will be established in righteousness.*

The heart of a King is in itself a vast unexplored vault; maybe that is why we have an urge to fill our hearts. The process of refining the minerals we find during our garden-extending reign is the same kingly process of removing corruption in favour of righteousness. Most of us know how glorious it is to reveal justice, to celebrate freedom and establish equity. It is the same inbuilt godly desire we have to find out more of the goodness of God; to meet him in the garden in the cool of the day, but to want more time with Him; to know him more deeply, to have his presence more fully, more often and in more places. Oh, the depth of the riches of the wisdom and knowledge of God! How unsearchable his judgments, and his paths beyond tracing out![44]

Our desire to find out more about our world, our galaxy and ourselves as human beings is the same desire we have to find out more about the One who made us. That is why there is no end to scientific exploration, artistic endeavour and religious expression. When we know more of God, we see and understand his creation more fully. When we search out his creation, we will be surprised at His majesty and creativity. Of course, there are those who simply see

---

44. Romans 11:33.

the world and its riches without observing the creator behind it and there are those who ignore the earth and miss its beauty in their pursuit of the divine.

The King and His Kingdom are inseparable. We experience the kingly rule of God and we experience the King himself. Exploring creation takes us to the heart of God and into His presence. There should never have been any dividing distinction between our mandate to fill the earth, and our desire for God's presence. It was never intended that the work of humanity on earth was somehow less than, or different to their worship of God. The Kingdom of God has always been about his reign and presence in relationship with mankind, and partnership with creation on the earth and in the heavens. The earth and the heavens were created together and God's intention was for a free, willing and loving humanity to join with their gracious God in bringing the fullness of his presence to the earth and filling the whole of creation in every way. In this sense, the paradise garden is not only the place where the Kingdom begins; it is also the first temple. God lives on the earth with Adam. The garden is the place where man meets God. It is the Holy of Holies; Eden, the Holy Place and the rest of the land, the Outer Courts. Everyone and everything is invited further in, even as God's presence bursts further out. Like Ezekiel's temple and the aqueduct of Solomon, there is a river running from the garden and so this house of God is also the source of life for everything around.

Selah, pause, reflect

What makes an espresso good?

To taste and touch, it is all down to the crema and the freshness if the beans.
To tend and grow, it is down to the cultivation and sustainability of the surrounding habitat.
To trade, it is down to the way the farmers are paid, the way the land and community treated, the transport, middlemen, traders, roasters and retailers.
A good espresso is a complex thing.

That is OK because God is complex and does complexity well. His Kingdom is his rule in a complex domain that fulfils his commands of justice, peace and joy for creation.

From Andrea Illy's book, *Espresso Coffee: The Chemistry of Quality:*

> Italian espresso is a polyphasic beverage, prepared from roast and ground coffee and water alone, constituted by a foam layer of small bubbles with a particular tiger-tail pattern, on top of an emulsion of microscopic oil droplets in an aqueous solution of sugars, acids, protein-like material and caffeine, with dispersed gas bubbles and solids.[45]

A good espresso is made as the hot water is subdued under pressure of at least 9 bars for about 25 seconds.

---

45. Illy, Andrea and Rinantonio Viani. *Espresso Coffee: The Chemistry of Quality.* Academic Press, California, 1995.

This leads to the water containing thousands of CO_2 bubbles, each of which have a strong surface tension due to the oils extracted. The freshness of the beans, the roasting process, the length of time, the temperature of the water and the length of the pulling of the shot all contribute to the drink and especially its 'crema', which ideally should hold a spoonful of sugar on its surface for a couple of minutes. Plenty of ruling and subduing going in here, with a need for the planning that comes from forming, before the drink is ready to enjoy.

It may taste good, but where are you drinking it and with whom? Does this make a difference? Is it a good coffee if you know that the people who have made it possible are in slavery? Does it taste better or worse, knowing that the land where it is grown has been consistently abused through chemicals and over-use? It can have a great crema and be a product of some well-formed thoughts, but as the product of a corrupted subjugation, it may not be a fully good coffee. It is also possible to drink a great cup but have no-one to enjoyably share the experience with. And it is possible to drink a coffee with no crema, and no sugar, that has not had enough pressure; but as it is drunk with friends, or with those who have grown it, we taste and see that it is good.

Good stuff needs to be subdued and ruled. Its production also needs to have been cultivated and protected well. How do we measure the goodness of our producing, without eating of the fruit of the tree of the knowledge of good and evil and holding our own personal benchmarking rod?

Only God knows. Only he can see how the Kingdom has been manifest. Only he can measure the thousands of variables that make up Good. But that shouldn't stop us from joining Him in this and growing in stature and wisdom and favour in our pursuit of a Kingdom of Heaven rule.

Heaven on, with, alongside, coming to, filling, touching, resting upon Earth

Genesis 1 and 2 contain within them the seeds of the Kingdom. The elements, commands, attributes and habits are all established in these early days. We know, shocking as it is in chapter 3, this plan is attacked, the earth is corrupted, authority is given away and mankind is shamefully cut off from that restful relationship with God. The next 1185 chapters are all about God's plan to restore this Kingdom. They describe His new plan to rescue the world, through the life and death and resurrection of the Servant King Jesus. And then there are two final chapters, at the end of the book of Revelation, that correspond to the first two chapters of the Bible in Genesis. In fact, it is almost as if the in-between chapters should not be needed. The Kingdom is established in Genesis and fulfilled in Revelation. But God's Kingdom plan, developed through Abraham, Jacob, Moses, David and the men and women of faith, is not a botched plan B. Finally, through Jesus, the first plan of Genesis 1 and 2, where the earth is filled with the knowledge of the glory of God, is back on track and completed in Revelation 21 and 22.

Revelation 21 to 22:5 is a vision of the Kingdom of Heaven fully on the earth. There are of course a few verses that refer to the experience of brokenness and subsequent healing of Jesus, but most of this vision would make sense even if there had been no fall of man, nor wars or sickness. It reads as the most wonderful response to the call of Genesis 1 and 2.

The mystery and yearning of the heavens – the skies and universe, the spiritual realms of Angels and the dwelling place of God – is finally satisfied, as the New Jerusalem comes down from heaven. As we have seen, our longing as we look at the night skies or the freedom of the birds is that there is a source of life just beyond our grasp. These days, scientists are looking into the very far off heavens for answers to the genesis of life on planet earth. We cannot help but look to heaven, to the beyond, or to the high majestic hills, where our help will surely come from as the psalmist sings.[46] And contrary to some theologies we have developed about escape, avoidance or snatching away rescue, the answer to our longing does not lie in us travelling away to these heavenly places, but in the mystery and power we sense in these realms being revealed and received here on the earth. Classically, this usually happens on earth in a temple; the garden being the first temple of God. But now there is no need for a special building or a special garden. The Lord God and the Lamb are the temple. God, who was walking with Adam and Eve in the garden, is now invited and welcomed by the people who have grown to know Him and love Him, to live fully among them at all times in all places. There is a shout of joy in heaven that says: Look, God's home is among his people! He will live with them, and they will be his people. God himself will be with them.[47]

This is the language of people; individuals and community. The earth of Genesis 1 and 2 was never a sterile complex laboratory experiment. Instead it was a young, fragile and malleable place which, given time and love, would grow

---

46. Psalm 121:1
47. Revelation 21:3.

up into the dwelling place of God and people. God gives us the gift of time so that we can grow in wisdom, stature and favour with God and man.[48] Such growth means that the earth can finally grasp the wonder of the heavens across the span of what was intentionally separated, and "the two shall become one".[49]

This is the phrase used at the end of Genesis 2. Male and Female have been fashioned from the same clay but separated out. The wonder of sexual consummation is the reconnecting and deep knowing of what has been apart. The preparation of that first bride and groom is their maturing in awareness of who they are and how they can love another. In Revelation, the image of husband and wife is picked up once again. This time it is Jesus, the eternal Son who lives at the right hand of the Father in the heavens, who is the husband. The people gathered together who have been loved and cared for, washed and dressed, are the bride. The marriage we glimpse between two individuals in the beginning is just the start. The plan was to have an ultimate marriage: for the bride who was earthly and has now grown up, woken by love having felt the breath of Spirit on her face, and for Her groom who rejoiced at her creation in the beginning. It appears that God created people to look after his earth and to discover his love, so that one day they would know this love fully and completely.

Heaven and earth. Heaven on earth. Just as Jesus spoke about the Spirit of God given to us in John 14, so heaven with earth; heaven alongside earth; heaven in earth.[50] This

---

48. Luke 2:52.
49. Mark 10:8.
50. John 14:16-17.

73

is why the Kingdom is always talked about as coming or arriving. We don't have to build a tower to reach the skies, but instead live in such a way that we invite heaven to fill the earth. This is the picture given to us in Revelation. God brings the Kingdom of the heavens to earth, in the form of the new Jerusalem, and, as usual in the economy of God, we fill it with who we are and what we have formed.

The garden is now a city, a place where many people can live. The city has been built: planned, formed and fashioned out of the same precious stones and metals found around the garden. In Genesis 4, we read about the beginnings of industry, farming and cultural expression.[51] The story of the Bible is then packed full of exciting stories about craftsmanship, building, technology and the arts. The first person to be recorded as being filled with the Holy Spirit is Bezalel, who is especially gifted in crafting the precious stones and fabrics for the tabernacle, elements later glimpsed in the New Jerusalem. Now there are more than just two people reigning on the earth. The Kings of the earth come into the new city and bring with them the glory and the honour of the nations. All that has been made, formed and subdued. All the ideas and discoveries. The arts and crafts. The food and fashions and languages of the cultures of the earth. All the good ruling and subduing that has multiplied and become fruitful now fills the new Jerusalem. None of this has been wasted. The Genesis project was not a futile experiment, but, like artworks thought lost after a great war, the wealth of nations is on display and built into the city.

51. Genesis 4:2-22.

The city has been measured, judged and ruled, both on earth by people and in heaven by angels. It is a curious combination of the physical and spiritual. Both spiritual and physical realities are important and honoured and are brought together in this city. Earthly things are not necessarily sinful, or somehow carnal, or just less-than shadows of other worldly ideas. Neither are spiritual things too lofty and ethereal or optional extras for the use of religiously inclined people. In this city, what has been measured and weighed, whether it is earthly or heavenly, is now built together. Even today it is often hard to distinguish between what is earthly and what is heavenly. How does music stir us? What design causes our souls to leap? Why do I feel so very satisfied, sitting under my vine with my neighbour in the cool of the day? Bringing up children, learning to ride, the smell of new emulsion of a clean wall, the speed of the motorbike and the fit of the dress. So many of our experiences are wonderful and yet so many are also tarnished, compromised and knottingly tangled that extricating them is a hopeless task. All these things and activities that bring life are redeemed by God. Everything that is designed in heaven and on earth forms the city. The fire of God's passionate love manages to burn off the dross, and its heat can even reorder what good and evil has seemed to irreversibly fuse together. There are no tears or sadness, oppression or slavery. The earth is not abused and scarred. And what we do, what makes each of us who we are, is a part of the glory and honour of nations on parade.

The City has walls, like the first garden, with open gates and free access to the north, south, east and west. And therefore, just like the first garden, there is a city centre. This is not for thrift shops or statues of bloodthirsty historical heroes. From the throne, down the middle of the street, flows the river of life, crystal clear and satisfying thirst at no cost. The tree of life, also, somehow either side of this river, nourishing and healing the nations. Jesus, the tree of life, God's wisdom and word; Jesus, the water of life and also Jesus, the light of the world. Shining all around the city is the light. There is no need for the governing and defining of the sun and moon. The spiritual reigning has now come to earth through the Lord God and the Lamb, the light of the world. It is the Lamb, Jesus, who is in the middle, glorious and majestic, yet a humble servant.[52] One who has truly demonstrated what it means to protect and serve. One who spat on some dust and formed new eyes. One who has built a new people, a house of living stones. This was God's greatest and most wonderful secret to be searched out in Genesis: for people to rule and reign and in doing so to find that Jesus the Son is the perfect image of the invisible God. God's intention all along was that their kingly serving, and divine imitation, would mean that they are conformed to the image of his son.[53] In Revelation 22 we find that we are in fact God's servants and through Jesus, his friends also, and with Him, we will continue the Genesis 1 Kingdom of God reign forever and ever.[54]

---

52. Revelation 5.
53. Romans 8:29.
54. Revelation 22:3-5.

Part I

The genesis and consummation of the Kingdom – epilogue

And so we know the beginning in Genesis 1 and 2, and we know the end of that beginning or the full establishing of a new beginning in Revelation 21 and 22. We were created to rule and reign in the Kingdom of Heaven and the future is looking bright. What we face, however, is how to live between these two beginnings. How do we continue the first Kingdom mandate in the context of brokenness, toil, groaning and resistance? How can we continue to rejoice in the day we were first created and the free command we were first given to be fruitful and multiply, when what spreads from us is often virus not virility?

In the next section we will look at what has attempted to derail God's Kingdom plan and the effect it has on us as stewards and rulers. We now reign in a world that is contested. Toil, pain, selfishness and ultimately death snatch away from us the joy of living in the new heaven on earth dominion. Which is why Jesus came to declare a new Kingdom, different to the corrupted one we experience through current human rule; one which would restore the original plan of God for His people and His earth. He came to earth to hands-on show us how to live this way and prove it is possible for a human being to live in death-free holiness. He proved this by revealing to us once more that this Kingdom is at its heart a kingdom of love and not power.

In fact, its power is held entirely by its love, and to gain this Kingdom, we need to lose our lives. This is counter-cultural to a race that has learned to self protect and self promote, but it is entirely congruent with a Genesis 1 and 2 Kingdom culture of service, joy and loving relationships.

And in the meantime we are still called to transform a garden into a city. We can use the boundaries, resources, examples and relationship with one another and with God to do this over time. It is supremely an activity of love and not just power or force or even hard work. There is a huge amount of human activity that fulfils this first command of the King, and just as Wisdom delighted in the loving work of the Father, so Wisdom delights in our own imitation of this work. There is a profound worship of God going on when a human being is subduing and ruling wisely, creatively and compassionately. In the face of poverty and pain, it is extraordinary how human beings have the capacity to find joy, to love and be loved and to enjoy the life given them.

The Spirit of God continues to brood over the surface of the deep, even when that sea is in turmoil. Although God's eternal power and character may sometimes seem invisible, from the beginning of creation he has shown what these attributes are like, by all he has made.[55]

We continue to reign in this contested Kingdom as we subdue with care and rule with wisdom.
Our care for the planet and its inhabitants can be characterised by our serving and protection.
We can fill the earth with what we have formed and built, using justice and compassion.
Our creativity displays the ingenuity and artistry of God.

---

55. Romans 1:20.

Now is not the time to ignore these God commands in order to avoid the traps and mires of strife and selfishness. Instead, our worship of God is beautifully displayed in what we do, how we do it and for whom we do it. To all teachers, medics, artists, engineers, farmers, administrators, managers, athletes and dog groomers: there is a stunningly beautiful city to be built.

Part 2

Shalom

Shalom

The Old Testament (and the Old Testament God) is renowned for its violence, battles, purges and general quarrelling and bad behaviour. It is also well known for poems and passages of peace and comfort that, in the English translations at least, have helped to form culture and language through generations.

If the first two chapters of Genesis are about God's plan for the Kingdom of His heavens to be fully experienced on the earth through people, their work and relationships in a growing partnership with Him; then the rest of the Old Testament is about His plans to still see this happen, despite the corrupting of those relationships and that work, and the breaking of partnership between God and mankind.

Genesis 1 is poetry, and Genesis 2 a tender, moving and mythically styled account of the act of creation. We see everything set in motion, but don't see how these plans for the glory of God to cover the earth may actually be realised. This is up to our (and Adam and Eve's) imagination. Genesis 3 is the tragic shattering of all that was sung and performed in the chapters before. Nevertheless, the Bible still manages to describe and point to where God's Kingdom rule is being revealed, even in the midst of thorns and thistles, pain and toil. The imprint of the King may be tarnished, but has not vanished from His image and likeness. Pain and toil have increased, and death and anti-Kingdom hang heavy in the air, obscuring the view of the clouds and heavens beyond. But there is a promise that breaks in through the misery and rain, and keeps breaking in time and time again, that this is not the end of the big Kingdom plan.

What breaks in, both in the biblical account of mankind's attempts to regain heaven and in our own experience and the experiences of cultures down the ages and across the globe, is the hope for peace. And by peace, we don't mean only an absence of war, nor simply a quiet field of butterflies, homemade lemonade and crisp linens. Peace is the Sabbath that God made, which leads to all kinds of ingenuity, creativity, passion and purpose. Peace is the justice of honouring, serving and co-operating with one another. It is the rest that contemplates a job well done, and begins to muse of new endeavours. It is the ability to fall asleep in contentment and wake up with the thrill of desire. Peace is the way tribe, family and tongue work together, honouring and celebrating one another. It is the jazz and polyphony of colours and sounds and smells and textures and voices. It is the drink in the late afternoon with our neighbours (who we may not even know, or as yet speak the same language) sitting under our fig tree and vine.

In spite of the undermining of God's Kingdom plan in Genesis 3 it is clear that its purpose of peace runs through creation and time. There is a word in the Bible that defines this peace and could be the description of what the culture of the Kingdom of Heaven is like in reality. This word is Shalom.

According to the Brown Drivers Briggs definition of the word Shalom it has a variety of meanings:
Shalom of course has a meaning as the peace from war, for instance in Psalm 120:7: "*I am for peace, but when I speak, They are for war.*"

Shalom is also completeness in number, and wholeness in system, as in the 'whole' of a people group in Jeremiah 13:19: *"All Judah has been carried into exile, Wholly carried into exile."*

Isaiah 32:16-18 is an amazing description of Shalom as the tranquility that comes from justice:

Then justice will dwell in the wilderness
And righteousness will abide in the fertile field.
And the work of righteousness will be peace (Shalom),
And the service of righteousness, quietness and
confidence forever.
Then my people will live in a peaceful habitation,
And in secure dwellings and in undisturbed resting places;

The justice of God's rule and reign is further described in verses like Psalm 85:10: *"Lovingkindness and truth have met together; Righteousness and peace have kissed each other."*

Shalom means welfare — we would ask how people are doing physically, socially, financially — Both Joseph and David are asked by their fathers to enquire after the welfare-shalom of their brothers.[56]

The welfare in Psalm 37:11 is translated as prosperity: *"The humble will inherit the land And will delight themselves in abundant prosperity."* The welfare-shalom of the city that Jeremiah calls the exiles to seek in Jeremiah 29:7 infers economic and cultural prosperity and a society of justice.

It means physical health and longevity in Psalm 128:6 and being 'well' is the exchange between Elisha and the Shunammite regarding her family in 2 Kings 4:26.

---

56. Genesis 37:14, Samuel 17:18.

Shalom also means the covenant of peace between people and God as seen in Isaiah 54:10, and in the well-known prayer of Aaron in Numbers 6:

The Lord bless you, and keep you;
The Lord make His face shine on you,
And be gracious to you;
The Lord lift up His countenance on you,
And give you peace.

Selah, pause, reflect

Spend some time reading and rereading the blessing of Aaron.

As you allow these words to rest in your soul, the breath of God articulates his love and blessing and forms his desires for you and in you. Listen and live for a few minutes.

The Kingdom of Peace
is a Place called Shalom

Shalom does not have to be only defined in its relationship with the conflict, sickness or poverty it may replace. Shalom is the very nature of the Kingdom of Heaven, and would always have been, even if there were no fall of man. Because of this, it is not like a fire extinguisher, or a throat lozenge that is only taken in case of emergency or pain. Such things are useful to have to hand but we hope we don't have to use them. Shalom has a different nature to this. Shalom is the bonfire night where there are no accidents, but where there are fireworks, hot chocolate and toffee apples. Shalom is the experience of health in the throat, where we can speak, sing, eat and drink normally and gladly. Shalom is a peace and rightness in all kinds of areas – physical, mental and spiritual health and wholeness, justice, relationships, welfare and prosperity. It is because of our scarcity or conflict in these areas that we assume this Kingdom is just an antidote or balm, whose qualities are only experienced or looked for as a remedy or therapy.

Therefore, Shalom has existence even in paradise. In fact, Genesis 1 and 2 gives us insight into what constitutes Shalom. The order given to the forming and the filling, the separating and the gathering, the earth, sky and sea habitats and their creatures, mean that there is a righteousness and justice about the planet. Injustice is where order and placing are violated. We sometimes assume that justice is only needed to impose order and punishment on potential injustice. The fact that there is no injustice in these days of creation does not mean that there is no active justice either. The command to mankind to protect and serve is the command for justice. Even in a sin-free environment, justice is celebrated and worked on. A wise judging, where Jesus is at the centre rather than our own arrogant judgementalism, will bring flourishing to Adam and Eve's garden and beyond.

The rhythms of evening and morning; God speaking; the 'Letting'; the confirmations of 'And there was . . .'; the 'God created's and 'God made's: all reflect the wholeness of a breathing heart-beating body both in action and at rest. Shalom is not a frozen stillness or an unmoving impassive soul. It is the living and breathing of an individual, a community and indeed a planet and cosmos. The Sabbath rest of God on the seventh day is the time, state and place of rest where he dwells and into which he invites us.

> *"Thus the heavens and the earth were completed, and all their hosts. By the seventh day God completed His work which He had done, and He rested on the seventh day from all His work which He had done. Then God blessed the seventh day and sanctified it, because in it He rested from all His work which God had created and made. This is the account of the heavens and the earth when they were created, in the day that the Lord God made earth and heaven."*

Although those first verses of chapter 2 act as a hinge and crossover for chapters 1 and 2 in their different styles and perspectives, the revealing of Sabbath in the narrative before the command to cultivate and guard tell us that the work of humanity is done from rest and peace. Sabbath rest is the context of the Kingdom of Heaven. It is the place of faith, where we cease from our work and trust that everything will be OK. Even going to bed is not easy when there are deadlines to meet and exams to revise for. Shalom is the non-anxious approach to living with responsibilities.

Shalom does not deny responsibility. In fact, true Shalom is where work is being done, but it is not toil or labour. Instead it is the joy-filled work of loving mercy, acting justly and walking humbly with God. There is plenty of responsibility in both the garden and the city of God. This is probably because of the emphasis that Shalom puts on relationship. First of all we have relationship with God. He creates us and cares for us, he gives us commands and promises for life and he meets with us with intimacy and insight. We are stewards on His behalf, which is a huge responsibility. We also have relationship to the rest of his creation, which we must rule over well and bring that creative pressure in order that the creatures, land and plants may praise God in their fitness. And we have relationship with one another. In a definite act of separation and then union, men and women are to correspond to one another in their loving and working.

Because of experience, our actual starting point is a life of scarcity, pain, evil and death. We long for a different kind of ruling than the ruling of despots, dictators and other people like us. However, it is important to begin with the Shalom of the Kingdom of Heaven rather than see it as simply a solution dreamed up by God in the panic and stress of the war room. While it is true that the Kingdom is coming to once and for all to destroy the evil kingdoms of this world, it is actually the case that evil first came against the pre-existent peace of the Kingdom of Heaven; a kingdom which was already in place and fulfilling its destiny.

The Kingdom of Heaven is Plan A. Evil came to thwart it. But Jesus, the King of Shalom, has restored this Kingdom back to its rightful place on the earth and in the heavens.

Shalom is the way of life that God enjoys and wants us to enjoy on the earth. It is written into the rhythms and orders of creation. Shalom is the earth's habitat and the whole point of it all. Shalom is all about living with justice, friendship, health and prosperity – and the thorough enjoyment of this. As the Bible story unfolds, we see families flourish, towns and cities being built, food grown and eaten, feasting tables of inclusion, stories of love and friendship, homes of welcome, town-squares of justice and workplaces of prosperity. This was always God's plan for the earth. That it would be filled, and then ruled well. Certainly, the manifestation of this will look different in various geographies, and among various peoples, but the Middle Eastern images, metaphors and historical accounts we read about in the Old Testament are easily understood by all peoples.

Selah, pause, reflect

When have you experienced Shalom in the last few weeks? Did others experience it with you, and did you all acknowledge the rightness of the moment?

Bring to mind a place, activity or group of people that speak to you of Shalom. What qualities do these times have that speak to you of Shalom? How do you see Jesus in these experiences?

Pictures of Peace:
Everything beautiful in its time

It is often the imagination of the prophets that describes how this peace-filled Kingdom will look, but it is also found in the work of the artists and craftsmen, in the rule of the Kings and in the many interventions of God, as the clouds of his home begin to brush the earth with their dew. Some of the most prominent metaphors and Kingdom experiences are to do with homes and towns, food and drink, the beauty of materials and design, the ordered joining of presumed opposites, and of course, the sound of singing.

Vine and Fig

A classic image is the Vine and the Fig Tree.

"Everyone will invite their neighbour to sit with them under their vine and fig tree."[57] The peaceful Kingdom of Solomon is described in these terms. Both Micah and Zechariah, in their imagining what the Kingdom will one day be like, pick up this image.[58] It is a beautiful metaphor, but also an actual activity, in an actual place for actual people. It is what people save up for to go on summer holiday. It is the picture of the good life in home décor magazines. Patio furniture, conservatories, barbeques and garden centres are all expressions of an industry that knows this is what the Kingdom actually feels like. Nevertheless, to enjoy

---

57. 1 Kings 4:24.
58. Micah 4:4, Zechariah 3:10.

Micah and Zechariah's vision, there has to be a peace in the land like Solomon's peace. It is hard to sit under a fig tree with the bailiffs at the door, or fever raging, or bullets flying. Or, wonderfully and ironically lived out by Jesus, there has to be faith in Sabbath, sitting under the tree while all that violence shouts around, to begin to experience the Kingdom even when the Kingdom has not yet fully arrived.

Sitting with a neighbour eating figs and drinking wine does sound like a holiday in the Mediterranean. It is a sign of the Kingdom of Heaven that we can enjoy even now, but on its own may make the Kingdom look too static. It is enjoyable, but at some point the eating of figs will mean you need the loo, and the conversation with your neighbour may well become slightly bonkers if there's only wine to drink.

Street Scene

Zechariah also imagines a city where there is some recreation and activity.[59] Old men and women will enjoy being surrounded by people, not shut away in homes, but out on the streets in safety, at the heart of the fun. Children will be playing in streets, not scared, or fighting or begging, or threatening. Their playing and skating and music and dancing and BMXing are all happening in the same streets where the elderly are eating fruitcake, crown green bowling and doing bingo. It is an image of generations together in safety and at recreation. It could be taken straight from a Borough Council Community Plan.

The city is made of houses, and Jeremiah's cry to Israel in exile is to build houses and plant gardens.[60] This is what

---

59. Zechariah 8.
60. Jeremiah 29:4-8.

it means to establish God's Kingdom on the earth. This is coupled with marrying and having children. It is the logical extension of Genesis 2. Isaiah also encourages houses and streets to be built in chapters 58 and 61, and Ezekiel then comes up with a whole city plan.[61] (And all these three prophets are describing it as happening in the midst of destruction and disappointment.) It is a place where everyone is involved and belongs. There are 12 gates that are always open for every tribe. There is plenty of land on the sides of the city for growing food. It is not that different from God's city planning that is given to Moses in the Book of Numbers.[62] As the people have increased and been fruitful, God allots land for them to settle into and cultivate. He also instructs the building of cities. These are urban centres where the Levites – the teachers, lawyers, architects, social workers, musicians – expressed and transmitted the culture of the people. These urban centres were bounded by common land, places of rest and recreation.

"Never again will there be in it
an infant who lives but a few days,
or an old man who does not live out his years;
the one who dies at a hundred
will be thought a mere child;
the one who fails to reach a hundred will be considered
accursed.
They will build houses and dwell in them;
they will plant vineyards and eat their fruit.
No longer will they build houses and others live in them,
or plant and others eat.
For as the days of a tree,

---

61. Ezekiel 40-48.
62. Numbers 35.

so will be the days of my people;
my chosen ones will long enjoy
the work of their hands.
They will not labour in vain,
nor will they bear children doomed to misfortune;
for they will be a people blessed by the Lord,
they and their descendants with them.
Before they call I will answer;
while they are still speaking I will hear.
The wolf and the lamb will feed together,
and the lion will eat straw like the ox,
and dust will be the serpent's food.
They will neither harm nor destroy
on all my holy mountain,"
says the Lord.

Isaiah 65:17-25 is a wonderful song that depicts the Kingdom of Heaven. In this passage and in many more, Jerusalem is the ideal city of the Kingdom. This is why its name is, literally, the City of Shalom. It includes once again the picture of homes and streets and buildings. In those places, the old and young mingle so you can't tell the difference between them. The gardens are full of vines, as ever, and there is the sound of rejoicing and those who were once enemies or separated will be joined together.

Perhaps this is why people love the magic of Christmas shopping, where the streets and town centres are open to all and the outdoor trading feels brighter, warmer and smells so good. The mini streets and villages of a music festival have a similar attraction. Visiting cities on holiday always feels more vibrant, fun and attractive because our guard is down and we're more likely to smile than wear the fixed frown of commuting or dashing to the dry cleaners. One of my fondest and most evocative memories from childhood is driving at night on the motorway past the city of Birmingham, in awe of the hundreds of street, house and factory lights, far away but beckoning to me to their life.

Feasting

Feasting is another everyday expression of Shalom. If we have done well in our cultivating and protecting and the garden is extending nicely, then there will be plenty of food for eating, which then prompts praise and thanksgiving. We have seen this as neighbours sit under vines and fig trees, but the bigger feast is a picture of joy, relationships, satisfaction and the fruits of God-inspired labour. God promises to give rains in their season and as this happens the land will yield its produce and the trees of the field will bear their fruit.[63] In a similar vision to Isaiah 65, Jeremiah 31 describes buildings and vineyards, but also a feast of music and singing and dancing; of old and young, men and women, where the grain, new wine and oil, the flock and the herd are evidence of the bounty and provision of God who hosts this Kingdom party.[64] The promised land is famously described as flowing with milk and honey. The blessing of God is experienced in this way:

He will love you and bless you and multiply you; He will also bless the fruit of your womb and the fruit of your ground, your grain and your new wine and your oil, the increase of your herd and the young of your flock, in the land which He swore to your forefathers to give

63. Leviticus 26:4.
64. Jeremiah 31:1-14.

you. You shall be blessed above all peoples; there will be no male or female barren among you or among your cattle.[65]

Isaiah 25 describes the day of the fullness of the Kingdom as a feast:

*On this mountain the Lord Almighty will prepare
a feast of rich food for all peoples, a banquet of aged wine –
the best of meats and the finest of wines.*

In Isaiah 55, as Jesus, son of David is revealed, God invites his people to eat:

*Come, all you who are thirsty,
come to the waters;
and you who have no money,
come, buy and eat! Come, buy wine and milk
without money and without cost.*

*Why spend money on what is not bread,
and your labour on what does not satisfy?
Listen, listen to me, and eat what is good,
and you will delight in the richest of fare.*

Theophanies, where the presence of God comes from the heavens and is clothed on the earth, are often marked by meals and hospitality. Whether this is Melchizedek feeding Abram, or Abram entertaining angels, or Gideon cooking for the angel, or even Peter on the rooftop invited to eat, the coming of the Shalom Kingdom is a meal with God Himself. Jesus of course teaches this many times, whether he is comparing the Kingdom to a wedding feast, feeding

---

65. Leviticus 7:13-14.

the five thousand or inviting his friends to eat a last supper with Him. In Revelation 3, the fulfilment of the Kingdom is the opening of the door between heaven and earth and the invitation from earth to Jesus in heaven, who will come in to our house and eat with us.[66] Psalm 23 has at its centre a feast and an overflowing cup prepared by God.[67] Our hosting of guests, whether they are family, friends or (especially) strangers is an expression of the Kingdom of Heaven. God is the ultimate host. These songs of praise and thanksgiving have this as their theme:

Psalm 36:8: *"They feast on the abundance of your house; you give them drink from your river of delights."*
Psalm 63:5: *I will be fully satisfied as with the richest of foods; with singing lips my mouth will praise you."*
Psalm 65:4: *"Blessed are those you choose and bring near to live in your courts! We are filled with the good things of your house, of your holy temple."*

Although our expectations of family meals or friends' parties can often be dashed by the reality of Auntie Gladys' wind, or cousin Colin's drunken curse, we often look forward to feasts and dinners with excitement and anticipation. We know, deep down, that they are meant to be good; ideally we could enjoy the friendship and the food and the drink. A true feast, with music and dancing, with fruit and wine, is the stuff of daydreams, usually glimpsed in movies and not always tasted in reality. But when it does happen, at a wedding, family meal, celebration party or impromptu celebration, we really do experience the

---

66. Revelation 3:20.
67. Psalm 23:5.

satisfaction of heaven. This is how life can be – without sickness, or loneliness or the alcoholic slide towards bitter honesty. Tapas, seafood, rhubarb and ginger meringue. Who wouldn't want to be fully human, made in the image of the feasting God?

Completing

Shalom is also expressed where opposites attract, or those that were separated are reunited, or where the ordering of God finds completion in the bringing together of that which was previously apart or even seemingly antagonistic. We have seen this already in Genesis 2, where the separating and defining of male and female then finds its fulfilment in sexual union. The heavens that were once apart from the earth will come down and both will be joined together. The animals that were ordered according to their kind find a peace-filled friendship. In Isaiah 11 and 65 the wolf and the lamb will lie down together. This is of course a strong metaphor for the banishing of fear, violence and prejudice, but it also declares that when the earth was created there was a trajectory, not just for mankind, but for the whole cosmos. This is a trajectory towards perfection, which is not blandness or a lack of creative tension, but a completeness where even the beasts are looking forward to a peace-filled habitat. What an amazing picture, of a toddler playing with snakes and no less amazing that those children should be safe enough to play together in the streets. Quite different to the danger of the snake in the garden or the rage of Lamech as he strikes a boy.[68]

---

68. Genesis 3:1, 4:23.

There are moments throughout the Bible story where the Kingdom completion of Shalom is glimpsed in its mad glory. Daniel is safe among lions; Jonah in a fish. A donkey speaks and a stick becomes a snake. Jesus walks on water, stills a storm and speaks to the wind and waves. In some bizarre and exciting way, the laws of nature we all respect and need are overturned by the King who first made those laws. Quite how this may happen is uncertain and mesmerising. But the Kingdom is a place where even the earth, stars and animals will be brought into completion; harnessed and subdued so that they may enjoy what their freedom in Christ's new economy really means. The psalms are full of this – 19, 65, 69, 96, 104, 145, 148, 150. The trees of the field will clap their hands and shout for joy. Leviathan plays in the ocean. The great sea creatures praise the Lord. The jackals and ostriches honour the Lord. The heavens declare the glory of God. The hills gird themselves with rejoicing. The hail and snow, the fruit trees and small creatures all praise the Lord.

Completion does not mean that everything is over and there is nothing more to do. It looks like there is plenty to do so the Kingdom is not ultimately boring, and its perfection and lack of pain does not mean that we will be without creativity or problems to solve. It could mean a whole new set of parameters, though. Maybe in its fullness there will be many more dimensions and laws. A newly released creation could be quite a handful for those of us who have become used to the earth imprisoned in its groaning. Certainly as we grab a hold of this coming Kingdom we might well glimpse more things in heaven and earth than are dreamt of in our more limited present philosophy.

Overflow and Blessing

We have seen that we may have a tendency to think of peace as a static absence of too much action or noise – a cul-de-sac or a final resting place. But Shalom is not this kind of resigned peace. It is joy and gladness peace as well as closing our eyes peace. It is the obvious friendship and peace between neighbours at a raucous street party as well as the quiet gratitude of a couple happily married for 50 years sitting side by side and watching the world go by. Shalom peace generates life. We may say that the impetus given to the earth and its creatures to be fruitful and multiply is an impetus to overflow.

Joel 2, that significant passage that Peter uses on the day of Pentecost, is a description of the Kingdom of Heaven exploding on the earth. The fig tree and the vine are once more used as an emblem of this new good life, and they are a comfort and sign, not only to humanity but to those animals that have been in fear, and to the land that has been bloodied.

> [21] *Do not fear, O land, rejoice and be glad,*
> *For the Lord has done great things.*
> [22] *Do not fear, beasts of the field,*
> *For the pastures of the wilderness have turned green,*
> *For the tree has borne its fruit,*
> *The fig tree and the vine have yielded in full.*

Satisfaction that comes from grain, new wine and oil has already been promised in verse 19 and then the prophet says in verse 23 and 24: *"Rejoice and be glad . . . The threshing floors will be full of grain,*
And the vats will overflow with the new wine and oil."

In Proverbs 3:10 this overflow of barns and vats is the natural result of order and peace. In Leviticus 26 God reiterates that this is His Kingdom way of doing things on the earth. The blessing will mean we haven't finished eating last year's harvest before this new one is ready.[69] Similarly, Amos prophesies that the "the reaper will be overtaken by the plowman and the planter by the one treading grapes. New wine will drip from the mountains and flow from all the hills".[70]

A key image for the Kingdom of Heaven is not a silo or reservoir where scarcity is protected and fearfully conserved, but a river. The river, which we see in the garden and then in the new garden city is a great image of flow and overflow. When God promises to cause rivers to flow in the desert, for instance in Isaiah 41 and 43, this is not only about quenching a thirst. It represents the continual blessing and resource of God. In Ezekiel's vision of Temple and City, the river which flows from the door of God's house is one that fulfils Genesis 1 as it is full of swarms of fish, has life wherever it goes, causes trees to flourish and be fruitful, and provides a place for mankind to do some subduing and ruling with their nets.[71]

The word often used to describe God's Kingdom culture of overflow is 'blessing'. In Genesis 1 God blesses the fish and birds and says to them to be fruitful and to multiply. He begins a movement towards overflow. He then does the same with men and women.

The idea of encouraging reproduction and creativity is to expect an exciting diversity, productivity, excellence and

---

69. Leviticus 26:2-12.
70. Amos 9:13.
71. Ezekiel 47.

abundance. This overflow does not end up in stagnant pools, or butter mountains, or self-storage units for addicted consumers. Each time this overflow of blessing is mentioned the result is praise and gladness. This shows us that praise of God is a part of the Kingdom's ecology, rather than the required obligation of a devout religious person. Praise is the expression of a blessed earth and sky. The trees and animals cannot help but praise God, any more than the sun, moon and stars.

> [9] *You visit the earth and cause it to overflow;*
> *You greatly enrich it;*
> *The stream of God is full of water;*
> *You prepare their grain, for thus You prepare the earth.*
> [10] *You water its furrows abundantly,*
> *You settle its ridges,*
> *You soften it with showers,*
> *You bless its growth.*
> [11] *You have crowned the year with Your bounty,*
> *And Your paths drip with fatness.*
> [12] *The pastures of the wilderness drip,*
> *And the hills gird themselves with rejoicing.*
> [13] *The meadows are clothed with flocks*
> *And the valleys are covered with grain;*
> *They shout for joy, yes, they sing.*[72]

This kind of overflow is the opposite of poverty's hoarding or fear's greed. We tend towards keeping what we have gained just in case we can't replace it or it gets stolen. We suddenly rush to buy sprouts at Christmas because they may run out. We are all too aware of the seemingly

---

72. Psalm 65.

finite amount of love or patience we have in our hearts. Wasting a pound coin that is swallowed up by a parking meter aggressively confronts our inbuilt desire to conserve what we have. The chocolate bar that we were saving is casually and probably not even very enjoyably eaten by our rival fridge raider. These things offend our instinct to save. Nevertheless, when we deliberately give away the good stuff, our hearts often register the Kingdom delight in generous living.

As God is moved to bless his earth towards overflow, there is the implication of him bowing towards earth. The Hebrew word to bless also means to kneel; it is the act of giving a gift to another on bended knee.[73] The nature of Creator God is love and humility, which is why he 'lets' creation get on with what it does, and why he causes creation to reproduce after its own kind. He is not a command and control King. Rather he is a lover King who blesses by kneeling towards the tiny, vulnerable earth, even breathing into the man's nostrils. The power of this act of humble blessing is extraordinary! Life explodes and very soon the overflow begins.

It is no surprise then, that the praise that results from this overflow is also a kneeling, bowing kind of praise, this time back towards the Creator God. So our worship is often described in the Old Testament using a word that means to bow or become prostrate.[74] How else can we meet with our kind, blessing-kneeling God who has caused overflow and riches, but to bow down before him in praise and worship? And as human beings empty their hands and let their hearts be filled with gladness and thanksgiving, then there is even

73. Psalm 95:6.
74. Psalm 95:6 (as well!)

more room for further blessing! It is exhausting to think about it! Actually, it is the polar opposite of exhausting. Rather it is replenishing.

Great Stuff

If we are influenced by the Georgian or Romantic poets then our yearning will be for a pastoral kingdom of horse and cart, butter churns, Gabriel Oak and Julie Christie. It is not surprising that many of our peace-filled Kingdom images come to us through pastoral poetry in the Bible, as David the psalmist was shepherd and musician as well as king.

Nevertheless, the Kingdom of Peace is celebrated through industry and craftsmanship as well as sunny days and babbling brooks. Shalom has a glory and beauty about it that is desirable and highly prized. Jerusalem, the city of peace, is described as "the perfection of beauty".[75] "Beautiful in elevation, the joy of the whole earth, is Mount Zion in the far north, the city of the great King."[76] In Ezekiel's story of love and betrayal, the woman 'Jerusalem' is described as having this outward beauty.[77] If Shalom were a woman, she would indeed be beautiful like Esther, and if a man he would be handsome like Joseph.[78]

Exodus 28 is a long and detailed chapter about how clothes should be made for Aaron for "glory and for beauty".[79] This work is to be done by skilled craftsmen who will have been especially endowed with spiritual wisdom by God. Kingdoms are ruled by anointed Kings. And the Kingdom of Heaven

75. Psalm 50:2, Lamentations 2.
76. Psalm 50:2, Psalm 48:2.
77. Ezekiel 16.
78. Esther 2:7, Genesis 39:6.
79. Exodus 28:2.

is ruled by God the King who, in turn has given authority to people to rule with Him. Here, that kingly anointing of authority is given especially to fashion designers. Bezalel the artist is reported as being filled with the Spirit of God for wisdom, knowledge and understanding in Exodus 31-38. His colleagues are described as having skill put in their skilful hearts by God.

This particular word for beauty, which describes Aaron's garments, is also used by David of the temple he wishes to be built for God. This word beauty is used by Isaiah of God who is a beautiful crown and glorious diadem for his people,[80] and of God's people who are a beautiful crown in the hand of God.[81] It is used, too, of the jewels given by God to the woman 'Jerusalem' in Ezekiel's story.[82] Their beauty is not just an outward appearance. In fact, in the Ezekiel story and elsewhere this kind of aesthetic can stumble and distract. But it is the combination of aesthetic loveliness and moral or even functional 'fit' that best describes beauty in the Kingdom of Heaven. It is the beauty of form and function. In fact, the beauty of the things of creation – flowers, trees, animals and people – is all about how they fulfil their place so perfectly. Beauty is not what has been airbrushed, but how something, as in Hopkins' poem, is itself, and of itself speaks. So, the same beauty of Aaron's clothes, the woman's jewels and David's planned temple, is the beauty of an older man's grey hair or a younger man's strength.[83]

The beauty and artistry of Shalom is often seen in how things that were different, or apart are now fitted in place.

---

80. Isaiah 28:5.
81. Isaiah 62:3.
82. Ezekiel 16:12.
83. Proverbs 16:31, 20:29.

This creative connectivity, seen at its most profound in our sexuality, means we can celebrate what is 'other' and also discover myriad ways to bind things together. That is why the wolf and the lamb may lie down together. It is why we may have both authentic and deceptive cadences in our music. It is why lime and chilli, or rhubarb and ginger work so well together. This beauty is fitting, even if it comes as a daring surprise. The Kingdom of Heaven is a place of invention and solution, in a way that is not simply utilitarian but somehow naturally obvious – even if we've never encountered such a thing before.

The kind of industry that characterises the Kingdom of Peace is one of skill, devotion, usefulness, ingenuity and a lack of greed or insecurity. What is best is that which is desirable and has value. But in a corrupted world, the goodness of beauty is sometimes twisted into a false God rather than a gift from God. Once again this is seen in Adam's exclamation upon seeing Eve; much value and desire is put on the beauty of sexuality, but often that desire ends up abused or abusing.[84] With similar imagery, the promised land has such value but God cries out in agony when this most treasured inheritance is trampled upon.[85] Hezekiah had a treasury of wonderful valuable objects and riches that, because of the pride of desire, he foolishly paraded before the King of Babylon.[86] "There is precious treasure and oil in the dwelling of the wise, But a foolish man swallows it up."[87] The fact that our culture celebrates a beauty that is often unreal and unattainable means that beauty can stumble us, annoy and depress us. This shouldn't mean that we strip

84. Genesis 3:16.
85. Jeremiah 3:19-20.
86. Isaiah 39.
87. Proverbs 21.

the church buildings of their architecture and hang drapes over our fat bottomed Reubens. It is natural for the pearl collector to sell everything to buy the prettiest pearl in the world. It is wonderful to celebrate the beauty of the athlete stretching over the hurdle, the 60's Aston Martin purring down Marylebone Road and the handcrafted wedding ring delicately placed on the bride's finger. Religion has tended to either amass riches and proudly outshine collectors and connoisseurs all over the world, or clamp down against beauty and repress it until it bursts out in rebellious high heels.

In God's Kingdom, however, these beautiful things are not a cause for abusing, boasting, wasting, or ignoring. What has value in God's eyes is truly beautiful and should indeed be desired. The wealth of nations – the culture, language, characteristics, science, art and engineering – is a characteristic of the Kingdom of Heaven. Not only do the kings bring this into Jerusalem in the book of Revelation, but God Himself "'will shake all the nations; and they will come with the wealth of all nations, and I will fill this house with glory,' says the Lord of hosts. 'The silver is Mine and the gold is Mine,' declares the Lord of hosts. 'The latter glory of this house will be greater than the former,' says the Lord of hosts, 'and in this place I will give peace,' declares the Lord of hosts."[88]

These constant glimpses in the Old Testament life of God's people – of patios and barbeques, of houses and parks, of good order and industry, of overflow and blessing, of art and beauty – demonstrate what peace actually looks and feels like in the everyday life of men and women. Shalom peace is the perfection of beauty – wearing gold and silver,

---

88. Haggai 2.

dressed in fine linen and silk, eating fine flour, honey and oil; the fruitfulness of the olive tree in the height of its season;[89] everything beautiful in its time.[90]

Selah, pause, reflect

Read Psalm 122 and meditate on Shalom in your own city.

I was **overjoyed** when they said:
"Let's go up to the house of the Lord."
And now at last, we stand here,
Inside the very gates of Jerusalem!
O Jerusalem, you were built as a **city of praise**,
Where **God and man mingle together.**
This is where all the people of Israel are required
To come and worship Jehovah-God.
This is where the thrones of kings have been established
To rule in righteousness;
Even King David ruled from here.
Pray and seek for Jerusalem's **peace**,
For all who love her will **prosper!**
O Jerusalem, may there be **peace** for those
Who dwell inside your walls,
And **prosperity** in your every palace.
I intercede for the sake of my **family and friends**
Who dwell there, that they may all **live in peace!**
For the sake of your house, our God,
I will **seek the welfare and prosperity** of Jerusalem.[91]

---

89. Ezekiel 16:13, 14 Jeremiah 11:16, Ecclesiastes 3:11.
90. T MacGonigal's work "Shalom Theology as the Biblical Foundation for Diversity" is not only an inspirational enquiry into the beauty of Shalom as explored here, but a comprehensive examination of Shalom across the whole Bible.
91. Psalm 122 (TPT).

The Violence of the Anti-Kingdom

The Kingdom of Heaven is seen in the paradise garden and then finally in the City of Peace. Genesis 3 to Revelation 20 describe for us the opposition of evil and the disorder that corrupts the Shalom-filled cosmos. The entry into the garden of the serpent, his lies and deceit – and the actions of humanity – change the scene totally and dramatically. Everything is corrupted. Although God's Kingdom does not change, nor the quality of Shalom, nor the incredible power of His love, they are now seen as different to, in tension with and even locked in opposition to just about everything we see and experience. This is why we are desperately looking for peace rather than basking in it as our natural state. It is why the qualities of the Kingdom seem so elusive, beyond our grasp and even impossible to handle when we do get to touch them. It is why we begin to see the Kingdom of Heaven as dreamlike and utopian, or frustrating, irritating and even downright wrong. For those in search of comfort, the Kingdom of Shalom does feel like a medicine or therapy. Our experience of it, however, is fleeting, tainted or diluted.

Genesis 3, and the subsequent chapters until God's Kingdom plan is seeded in Abram and Sarai's lives, reveal how corrupted the earth has become. The serpent undermines the first commands of the King. The Shalom of being at peace with one another, the earth and with God is broken by the crushing weight of trying to be like God, when we are already his image and likeness. There is no real Shalom if people are suspicious of one another and God, blame one another and God, hide from one another and God – which is what happened with Adam and Eve. Order is further broken when Cain's feast of thanksgiving turns into competitive insecurity, an angry heart and a field not of new grain but of blood. Lamech continues to distort what is beautiful and fitting by marrying and demeaning two women and declaring that his sexual and violent power will win the day rather than humility, trust and equality. Even the orders in the heavenly places break their ranks to spill out onto the earth as the sons of God take daughters of men and it is only a shortened life span that limits spiritual chaos on the earth.[92] In the story of Noah, we glimpse God's horror: "Then the Lord saw that the wickedness of man was great on the earth, and that every intent of the thoughts of his heart was only evil continually."[93] This seems to be one of the worst lines in the Bible, in literature even. When overflow of blessing was God's intention for His Kingdom, hearts are overflowing with evil instead.

This is not how God intended mankind to live. This is not the Kingdom of heavenly Shalom ruling on the earth. The plan was to cultivate the garden, to fill it and extend it, according to God's plans and initial plantings. Now they are locked outside of the garden in the jungle. It is not right for work to be so tough and the earth so unyielding. The antagonism between the serpent and the woman is an awful way to live. Men are not meant to turn on women and rule over them, their coregents. Nor are women meant to reach out at their husbands like sin reached out to trap Cain.

Nevertheless, these new barriers, hardships and violences do not mean that the Kingdom plan is redundant. God

---

92. These stories are found in Genesis 4-6.
93. Genesis 6:5.

himself makes clothes to cover Adam and Eve's shame and reinstate their glory. God himself pleads with Cain and then graces him with protection. And God himself, in the midst of such evil and exhausting corruption, has a plan. This plan is called Noah, whose name means Rest. It is the plan of Shalom that cannot be swamped by a flood of evil. Sabbath turns out not to be a retreat away from the world but a strategy to save the world. Through the flood act of cleansing, order is restored. There is a similar ordering of animals and separating of waters from land that we find in Genesis 1. There is the same command to the birds and the animals to be fruitful and multiply. And God blesses Noah, which is his overflow nature, and once again speaks life by repeating the command for Noah's family to be fruitful and multiply, to populate the earth abundantly and multiply in it. The rule of the Kingdom of Heaven is seen once more in the commands to honour relationships and the sanctity of life. We see the celebration of commonality of family but with difference in culture as Noah's sons spread out according to the order of their language, nation and land.[94]

From now on, the Kingdom of Heaven plan, for the knowledge of the glory of the Lord to cover the earth, will continue to happen. This is through the direct strategy of God in partnership with those men and women who experience His love and who, in turn, live in love for the King. But the Kingdom is now surrounded by opposition and battle. It is expressed in people and communities that are often broken, half-hearted and mistaken. Rather than the Kingdom being experienced only as a paradise, it is contested on the battlefield. This does not change the

---

94. Genesis 8:15-9:17.

nature of the Kingdom. It is still a kingdom of peace and love. Shalom is still its heart. God does not revert to power in order to violently oppress his enemies into submission (despite the way we sometimes read the Bible). Shalom is the end and Shalom is the means to that end. We'll see in Section III that the coming of Jesus is the coming of love; the embodiment of Shalom; the citizenship of the Kingdom rather than the conscription of empire. But fighting evil with love seems particularly foolish. Bizarre scenes of hippies armed with flowers come to mind, or a barrage of pink love-heart balloons sent to overcome enemy artillery. In reality, the lovers may get thoroughly beaten by the evildoers. Except that Shalom love *is* the power of God, and the earth and humanity were originally designed to run along the lines of such a kingdom. If this is truly the case, then perhaps it is possible to overcome evil by doing good. So we live in a tension. Deep down, most people on the earth know that the Kingdom of Heaven is what wonderfully works. Yet also deep down is a suspicion that in the process of it working – we may get left behind, or miss out, or be abused – so we have invented other ways to establish such a kingdom that puts a priority on our own position in its prosperity.

From Joseph Heller's masterpiece on crazy humanity at war, *Catch 22*:

"From now on I'm thinking only of me."
Major Danby replied indulgently with a superior smile: "But, Yossarian, suppose everyone felt that way."
"Then," said Yossarian, "I'd certainly be a damned fool to feel any other way, wouldn't I?"[95]

---

95. Heller, Joseph. *Catch 22*. London: Penguin, 1975.

It is too risky to stick to love if everyone else is going only with power. We may want to, and even enjoy it when we do. But on the whole we end up hedging our bets by hoping for the best but expecting the worst.

Selah, pause, reflect

When have you felt the tension in your stomach between revenge and forgiveness?
When has love won?
When has love been crushed by anti-Kingdom violence?
How should we then live?

For me, two images come to mind. Banksy's "Flower Thrower" or "Love is in the air", the figure of a rioter throwing a bunch of flowers rather than a Molotov cocktail; Jeff Widener's photograph of 'Tank Man', the student who stood in front of the tanks in Tiananmen Square on June 5 1989.

Family: Shalom's alternative to a government strategy paper

The story of Israel in the Old Testament is God's strategy to model the Kingdom as best as possible, and then, into that albeit dysfunctional model, to place a new Adam who will rule and reign well over creation and once again call humanity back into that regent role. When God is ruling in the midst, the earth flourishes. The story of the Old Testament is the story of God loving people so that they invite him to do just that, which in turn leads to Shalom living.

This Kingdom strategy does not begin with a palace and a throne room, but with a family. The Kingdom of Heaven is never a top down imposition of imperial rule but always the product of love for God and for one another. It is true that when God chooses Abram and his wife Sarai they are chieftains in a land of nomadic and settled tribes, but their story is about their family rather than their attempts at local political rule. God's promise to this childless couple has the same qualities as his promises in Genesis 1 and 2. It is a blessing that will lead to fruitfulness, multiplication and overflow. It is also a hint that what is seen as awesome and unreachable in the heavens above is actually God's plan for the earth below. Abraham and Sarah experience a realistically tough earthbound life, but one that is full of Kingdom of Heaven interventions. We have observed that the rule of the Kingdom has in its sights some completing and perfecting that appears physically impossible to us right now. For Sarah, she looked at her old, wrinkly and shrivelled husband and laughed in disbelief that he would once again be able to rip off his clothes and leap onto her bed. The Kingdom of Heaven often elicits this kind of scepticism, mockery or simple resignation. Whether it is Nicodemus, Thomas or those gathered round the cross, when we are firmly rooted in a world that seems stuck in inevitabilities, to enter the realm of prosperous Shalom requires faith.

Sarah's laughter, however, soon turns to joy and the son who is born, Isaac – meaning laughter – is a living reminder that the Kingdom of Heaven has the ironic, surprising, comedic inversion of the way things usually are at its heart. The Kingdom of Heaven is a comedy in that the kings are brought low and the donkeys rule. In fact, the comedy of the Kingdom is our strength. There is often an energy to joy that causes us to dance, to move, to wave our arms and pirouette with delight. The Bible recognises this and many of the words for joy used in the Old Testament have the implication of jumping, spinning, turning and dancing in their root meaning. Not only do people express their joy with loud shouts, songs, jumps and dances, so, too does the whole of creation. The whole of Psalm 96 is a song of energetic praising laughter:

> Let the heavens be glad (merry), and let the earth rejoice
> (spin round);
> Let the sea roar, and all it contains;
> [12] Let the field exult (jump), and all that is in it.
> Then all the trees of the forest will sing for joy.

This is not necessarily a reason for us to make Jewish circle dancing or Strip the Willow an integral part of our weekly religious ritual. Nor does it mean Patrick Swayze and Baby should be venerated as saints while the angels sing, "I've had the time of my life." But the spinning of the joyful earth is its gravitational strength, and the God who rejoices over us with shouts of joy is the Mighty Warrior in our midst.[96] Just as Nehemiah said to Israel, in the face of opposition, that joy was their strength, so it is written of the wife in Proverbs 31: "Strength and dignity are her clothing, And she laughs at the future." The Kingdom of Heaven has a way of turning crouching fear into a dance of delight, which is nothing short of miraculous.

The joy-filled intent of the Kingdom of God is revealed time and again into this family. The scene is usually domestic, but the experience is heavenly. There are feasts and quiet sitting-under-the-tree moments of satisfaction. There are dreams and challenges where the presence of God becomes more intense and personal even than those early walks in the garden in the cool of the day. There is hard work that is contested but also hard work that is rewarded and successful. There are traps and prisons, bonded labour and deceitful contracts. Shalom is the breaking free of chains and burdens that constrain and imprison. There is strife, bitterness and murderous intent but then the power of Shalom works its way through the family to a place where there is weeping and tenderness and such forgiveness, as if a brand new start is actually possible in the embrace between sworn enemy brothers.[97] Therefore it is no surprise that the Kingdom strategy of God has within it the dramatic release from all that entangles. As the family grows, it needs to learn from the King what it is to live in freedom and hope rather than to lock everything down, to

96. Zephaniah 3:17
97. Genesis 32 and 33

avoid pain, and to only contain and manage for the sake of conserving resources.

The family becomes a family of families, where the Godfather is God the Father.

The next stage of the strategy is to see whether, what can happen in one family, can happen in a family of families. The first experience of the Kingdom of Heaven for the family of families now called Israel is that of release from slavery. Ironically, the opposite of the Kingdom reign of human beings according to God's will, is not experienced as a wonderful freedom away from Him to enjoy doing whatever we like. Instead it is our own experience of being subdued and ruled over. Being bound and enslaved by the very earth and people who we were meant to be cultivating and guarding. So, if this is what we are born into, although the Kingdom of Heaven is still seen in our image of God-ness, the most dominant drive in us will be the drive towards self and autonomy. The Bible calls this sin. Sin enslaves us because although it promises what God is hoping to give us for free in the Kingdom, it flogs us cheap imitations at an impossibly high price. We still desire the Kingdom – for instance, the experience of sitting under our fig tree – but because we are worried that there may be only one fig tree for many of us, we fight for it like a game of musical chairs and then even gloat when we have pushed others out of the way. We'll still enjoy the figs for a while, especially if we are past caring about what we have done to others to get there, but there is not as much laughter as if we'd invited our neighbours to join us. And we soon get jealous when we glimpse them sitting under a magnificent Cadbury's Dairy Milk tree, dropping its buttons into their undeserving laps.

So, we start to wish for another world.

In dramatic rescuing fashion, God brought his people, this family of families, out of slavery and put into their imagination a vision of a good land. The look and taste of this was meant to spur them on in anticipation and excitement that not only were they free from slavery, but that there was a new way of living to be had that was fully fruitful. There is a longing and yearning, now as slaves or newly freed slaves, as we dream of a new life of abundant fruitfulness. The harsh strength of our experience on earth – of resistance, toil, pain and disappointment – means that this yearning is more often than not translated to another world or existence. The here and now appears impossibly resistant to the reign of God we read about in the first pages of Genesis. For Israel in the desert, the experience gap was such that they again longed for slavery. For many of us the gap has a similar effect. We lower our expectations and live a lesser kind of life and we then put our hope, not in the Kingdom of Heaven coming to earth, but in the fantasy of leaving the earth to live in what looks like a better place.

Instead of an escape away from a miserable existence, God's plan was to establish what the Kingdom of Heaven looks like, not just in a single family but in a family of families who are all experiencing a freedom from slavery and a new sense of identity as a large family with a new purpose. A Kingdom of Heaven society. It would seem relatively straightforward for Adam and Eve to fulfil the Kingdom mandate. There were only two of them to debate and dialogue and find agreeable solutions to the challenges of cultivating the earth. For Abraham's family, this was more complex. A mix of parents and the resulting bonds and strains of brotherhood meant that common aims and goals were sometimes achieved, in a courageous and moving way considering the tensions that were often around. However, the challenge of a commonality of purpose between many fathers, mothers and families is an altogether different thing.

What we see in the forming of Israel in the desert is that God's insightful laws, rituals and traditions reveal the Kingdom of Heaven as not simply about an individual's happiness or one option out of many that a family may choose to live by. The Kingdom of Heaven is a way of living that is for the whole family of Israel and indeed for all of humanity on the earth. It is the justice, peace and joy of Father, Son and Holy Spirit that blesses, fashions and beautifies a people. Although the world is still corrupt and even the people that God spends most time with are vulnerable and violent, he still goes ahead with creating a new Kingdom model. This is because love, which is at the heart of His reign, is actually more powerful and eternal than the deceit and curse of the serpent. Whenever there is a person who trusts in the love of God and then lives within this new family of families model of Shalom, then peace and prosperity begin to spring forth, and people, the earth and its creatures all begin to feel the benefit. There is a great series of stories in the Book of Judges where this happens. The setting is usually one of oppression and economic crisis, where a person is raised up who has eyes to see the God of Peace. They may just have a few small glimpses, but it is enough to turn a whole people around from hiding away in a pathetic version of cultivation and protection, to singing songs of what happens when women and men rule well and give of themselves freely.

First of all, the Kingdom of Heaven requires that God's presence is in the midst of the family. If his love and light are not there, then the cold and dark quickly overcome whatever sparks of life are known. The Kingdom of Heaven is where a group of people are living well on the earth and God is living there with them. It is more of God's transforming presence for each and all.

So instead of the one-on-one appearances to Abraham's family, or indeed to Adam and Eve, God is continually present with Israel in cloud and fire and in the tabernacle, demonstrating the ultimate plan to be living on the earth.[98] The tabernacle reveals God's Kingdom passion for materials and design and beauty; the creative pressure of the artist and craftsman. Living well is not only about economics and logistics, but beauty and atmosphere and culture. At the same time as spreading himself like a canopy over many people, his personal encounters become even more intimate and intense with Moses and Joshua. There is an increase in both breadth and depth to his presence, showing that his rule will not get thinner and thinner the more it is spread, but miraculously it will end up with more power and grace and prosperity than there seemed at the beginning. Once again this shows the overflowing of the Kingdom that is characterised by abundance and not scarcity.

---

98. Exodus 13:21,22

Selah, pause, reflect

What do you see in cultures today and in the history of mankind that reflect the Kingdom of Heaven?

When is it that people can only imagine a far off and heavenly beyond, rather than a transformation of the here and now? What, therefore, is our call to those people?

How possible is it today for one family's culture to transform many families' cultures? Where would you start, if you wanted to do this with your own family?

Shalom and Jubilee:
family fortunes

The kingdom culture that God establishes in this family of families is one of health, justice, friendship, forgiveness, prosperity and welfare. While they are in the wilderness, every aspect of life is dealt with: the disorder that has spread like a virus across the order of creation; the mismanagement of people, land, resources and animals; the brokenness of relationships, deliberate selfishness, or mistakes and failings and their consequent shame. This all culminated in the year of Jubilee which is about deep reconciliation.[99] Leviticus 25 is an extraordinary chapter of revolutionary living! It began on the Jewish day of atonement, rediscovering the "at-one-ment" we can have with God. Jubilee year extended this out not only to neighbours, but to foreigners and then even to the land itself. Jubilee is the overcoming of curse and death. It is God's trumpeted Kingdom decree that living in seventh day Sabbath and carrying this on even into the future of the eighth day is the true way to cultivate and keep. In Sabbath, the challenge is to not do any work but still trust that everything will be OK. In Jubilee, this rest is extended into a celebration of wonderful possibilities. If we truly rest, then it is possible that we will still be reaping the fruits of our labour once we get back to work over the next couple of years! In Jubilee, there is release from slavery for the land, the resources, the animals and the people. Growth in creativity and activity is exponential. Where

---

99. Leviticus 25-27.

five will chase a hundred, then a hundred will chase ten thousand.[100] Presumably ten thousand will chase five million, which would be a very big wide game.

Not only is God the architect of a spiritual and physical world, he is the architect of a culture. This Jubilee culture is his blueprint for humanity. It was given in the midst of stress, rootlessness and pressure, to a people who were looking for a city whose architect and builder was God. It looks idealistic and unreal and it is unclear how much of this was put into practice by Israel. But the full Shalom of Jubilee is what the prophets then spoke about and it is this call to Jubilee that Jesus lived out and articulated as the Kingdom of God. So Israel, the family of families, is an example of what life can be like when God is ruling in the centre and people are protecting and serving the earth and one another.

The Jubilee Kingdom is a rule where all the elements that prevent us from having peace with God or with each other are dealt with. The disorder that we see in people's lives and bodies and circumstances ultimately works against feasting and friendship Kingdom. The prophet Isaiah has a vision of what life could be like if these things were addressed once more, and he, too calls it the year of God's favour, the Jubilee. He identifies what conditions push us apart from one another and prevent the rule of the Kingdom of Heaven. They are all opposites of Shalom. In the Kingdom of Heaven the poor have good news given to them, the hungry are fed, the naked are clothed and the slaves are set free. The blind see, the deaf hear, the mute speak and the

---

100. Leviticus 26:8.

lame walk. The brokenhearted are healed, the mourners are comforted and the dead will rise.[101]

This is the recognisable heart of Shalom for us living in the earth now. Although Shalom is not simply the absence of war, it is seen in glorious relief to the reality of injustice that so many people face. Jubilee is justice. There is no real Jubilee if some are sipping iced tea on their patio while others are being beaten into harvesting that tea, or the earth is being beaten into growing it. Jubilee is strong and muscular. It is the spirit of God the warrior who defends the poor, the widow and the fatherless. The trumpet sound of Jubilee breaks the bow and cuts the spear in two.[102] Because of the power of this justice, swords and spears will be hammered, by much subduing, into farming implements for some cultivating. True Shalom justice means that everyone will walk in the same upward path rather than trip over into the valley of despair.[103] The Kingdom of Heaven has a beauty that is strong; has laughter that heals; has peace that is noisily fun. It is a justice that is not achieved by force, sanctions and bullying, but by love that wins the hearts of a very mixed bag of people.

Isaiah was not looking for a communist utopia where everyone would be exactly the same. He was declaring that the Family of God could find a way of looking after one another, even in the midst of difference. Jubilee is not a levelling into greyness and uniformity, but rather the ensuring that no-one is excluded from the feast. King David demonstrated this by inviting Mephibosheth, whose physical

---

101. Isaiah 58, 61.
102. Psalm 46.
103. Isaiah 2:2-4.

disability and family history had excluded him through fear and insecurity, to join with David at the palace table.[104]

This is Jubilee.

In fact, in the Kingdom where there is no suffering, we may well bring in the riches of all we have learned and appreciated even when we have suffered under pressure or been painfully forced into ingenuity and creativity.

This is redemption.

This will include the beauty and concealed depths of the cultures surrounding the blind and the deaf in sign language and braille, and the majesty and resilience of the physically disabled. It will include the songs of the slaves and the craftsmanship of the untouchables. In the Kingdom of Jubilee, all that has oppressed and made miserable is taken out, and all that is appreciated and beautiful – even in circumstances we may consider less than our ideal – is lifted up and celebrated.

Selah, pause, reflect

We don't live in a fair world, so we don't have Jubilee yet. Therefore, trying it out is a risk. But what if the trying out led to its arrival, rather than waiting for its arrival in order to try it out?

What would be a first Sabbath-Jubilee step for you to test God in his generous faithfulness?

How will you try it out this week?

---

104. 2 Samuel 9.

How on earth can peace-full family life have a chance in hell?

The next part of God's strategy is that this family of families acts as a many-gated demonstration into which any may enter and join in with what God is already doing. The Kingdom of David and Solomon is a kingdom like this, where anti-Kingdom is overcome and a government of peace is established that will then be a blessing to all the families of the earth. Such a new kind of kingdom that prospers and does good is in opposition to what is already in place. The story of the kings of Israel and Judah and their enemies is a story of battle and conflict.

The Old Testament is characterised by war and bloodshed. Yet, as we have seen, the whole point of the story of God in relationship with earth is the Kingdom of Shalom. The violence therefore is the resisting of this heavenly government. This means that even though the Kingdom brings peace, it is also a kingdom at war. The earth which was once characterised by a paradise is a battleground, territory which is fought over. It is not as simple as a few people setting up a new Eden on an island somewhere and starting again by being nice to each other. There are other kingdoms at work that undermine the Shalom rule of the God of Israel from within and mock Him from without. The Kingdom of Heaven is not easily established. Goodness and faithfulness are assaulted. What has been gained is not shared with generosity but ring-fenced and aggressively defended. There are increasing indications throughout the

Bible that the forces arrayed against the King of heaven are heavenly-spiritual themselves. The patterns of evil are more than just the same mistakes or self-centred actions repeated a few times. In the same way that order was broken when the sons of God came down to the daughters of men, so we see individuals moved by Satan, groups of people dedicating themselves to spirits of death and violence, and even kings and nations on earth influenced by darker spiritual forces bent on humiliating God by corrupting his beloved creation.

This is a real pain. If it were just me and my own rebellion that I face, or that of some opponents in close proximity, there may be a few clever little stratagems to avoid the conflict. But it seems that the Kingdom of Heaven is a bit like a multi-episode TV crime drama, where ever more layers of baddies and their corrupt systems are revealed until it seems futile for the hero to try to achieve anything. The helplessness of Neo in the Matrix or Winston Smith in 1984 presents an understandably pessimistic view of the human condition, where something (or even nothing) is so big and bad that we are inadequate to do anything.

Therefore, although we have seen that the Kingdom of Heaven is the way we are intended to live on the earth, it is also a spiritual kingdom that provokes other unseen powers, and the manifestation of this battle is then seen in sickness, injustice, poverty and hatred.

Finally in this family, an older brother, an heir, who looks like a son of man but lives like a son of God and rules like a true king.

The story of this spiritual conflict using earth as its battleground is brilliantly described in the book of Daniel.

This is fitting, as this book is written by a ruler; one who is skilled in politics and government, who has experience of subduing and reigning, of cultivating and keeping. Daniel is wise and in him we see an example of what a new Adam regent may look like, in a similar way to that other wise ruler Joseph. Daniel experiences the power of the Kingdom of Shalom in his own personal life, as he trusts in God for his health and welfare, and also as he connects deeply and personally with the presence of God through his imagination in order that the wisdom of heaven is perceived on the earth. He may work for a king who is an enemy of Israel, but he continues to be obedient to the mandate given to Adam and Eve to govern wisely and compassionately.

As he understands the nature of governance and rule in his career, so too Daniel begins to appreciate more keenly the nature of the governance of God and the battle of the Kingdom of Heaven with the kingdoms of the earth. These empires are not built on Shalom, but on power and control. In Nebuchadnezzar's dream in Daniel 2, there are Kingdoms that follow on from one another, from the Babylonian, the Medes the Persians and the Greeks-Romans. They are domineering and impressive, but each of them reaches a point where it is overtaken by the next. Finally, another kingdom is described. The God of Heaven will establish it; it is like a rock hewn out of the mountain that will crush all the others and will itself never be destroyed. In his lifetime, Daniel experienced the crumbling of one power base followed by the emergence of another. His conviction about the Kingdom of Heaven, however, was that it is rocklike in its resilience. This is an interesting attribute after we have observed it being a kingdom of peace, humility and love, which are often seen as fragile and even weak qualities. The nature of the Kingdom of Heaven continues to be revealed throughout the book of Daniel.

Nebuchadnezzar himself has a revelation of this Kingdom in Daniel 4. The beginning and end of the chapter have this announcement:

His kingdom is an everlasting kingdom
And His dominion is from generation to generation.[105]

So, the Kingdom of Heaven somehow overarches human history; the rule of God has been at work in every generation and will continue. It is not a new idea as a plan B for a world gone wrong, but an ancient idea that makes everything new. Another king that Daniel worked for had a similar revelation. Darius declares to his people in chapter 6:

For He is the living God and enduring forever,
And His kingdom is one which will not be destroyed,
And His dominion will be forever.
"He delivers and rescues and performs signs and wonders
In heaven and on earth,
Who has also delivered Daniel from the power of
the lions.[106]

Not only does the Kingdom of Heaven span all time, and rule over every other rule, but it has a powerful effect in heaven and on earth in the present. The Kingdom of Heaven is not simply 'up there' as a distant but relatively ineffectual reign, there are signs of it and its wonderful heavenly nature that break into space and time. It is real and relevant in the affairs of men, just as it is in heavenly realms.

---

105. Daniel 4:3.
106. Daniel 6:26-27.

In the next chapter of Daniel, it is he himself who has the vision and insight into the Kingdom of Heaven. This time he sees Jesus the Son of God, in likeness as a man (who he calls the Son of Man), similar to Adam and Eve who were in likeness to God. The Son of Man, like a new Adam, is being given the rule of the earth by God. It is the same Kingdom that will last forever and will not be destroyed. Now all the people of the earth who have been fruitful and have multiplied will serve this king. His rule, however, is not determined and bolstered by such service. Through the generosity and grace that characterises the humility of God's rule, He then gives this Kingdom to His holy ones, who will receive and possess it themselves even as He continues to have dominion.

This is a vision of the intention and fulfilment of Genesis 1. God the Father honours His Son, who was there rejoicing with Him in creation, by giving Him the Kingdom of Heaven. And this Son, out of reverence, love and respect for His Father, gives away this rule back to the people who were made in Creator God's likeness, who in turn continue to serve Him. Everyone in the vision seems to be exercising their power by sharing it and giving it away. This is not because they do not value it, but because honour and grace characterise a life of Shalom.

So, it seems, the Kingdom of Heaven was always meant to have the Son at its centre, whether as the tree of life, the river source of life, the word of God, the firstborn and first place in all creation. And the people who God created were always meant to steward this planet and reign in this Kingdom as coregents. As they were fruitful and multiplied and applied their creativity and work to the role given them, they would seek out their God and get to know Him, Father, Son and Spirit. His blessing of them would cause life to overflow and praise to erupt. And they would then bless the earth so it too would respond in praise and singing. In the end a city would be built, containing all the wealth of nations and so be filled with the presence of God.

This is the vision of the Kingdom of Heaven, seen at a time when the opposite was happening. The people of Israel were scattered and the anti-Kingdom of insecurity and pride ruled forcefully. Daniel was caught in between these two realities and the pressure of the two squeezed him, even physically and mentally. The age to come was still a prophesied promise, and the current age was full of violence and war. The tension of these two opposing kingdoms is one of the things that makes the Bible puzzling and the experience of faith bewildering. It is a tension groaned in the Old Testament that eventually will go on to cause a tear in every person, in creation and in the Creator Himself.

Part 3

Jesus and the Kingdom of Heaven

The Servant King of the upside-down kingdom

The theme of the Kingdom of Heaven is introduced by Jesus early on in his ministry in each of the four gospels. It is through Jesus that we hear this phrase and ever since it has either been ignored or interpreted in all kinds of ways. Jesus is, of course, most well known for dying on a cross and rising from the dead. This follows lots of stories he told, teachings he gave, works he performed and people he spent time with. Throughout Christian history these activities, including the talk of the Kingdom of God, have at times been separated from one another or graded into levels of importance and significance or given symbolic or spiritual meanings. Or Jesus' message is seen as somehow different to all that has gone before, almost as if he is a plan C (after the plan A of the garden and plan B of Israel). His message, often seen to be of a spiritual nature and aimed at individuals, is to find a life that transcends this one beyond space and time through the discovery of a new morality.

But it is more likely that Jesus used the phrase 'The Kingdom of God' to deliberately join himself with the rule that God gave to mankind in Genesis, and also the strategy of God bringing a reign of Shalom through families to the world. Jesus' Kingdom is not different to these, but is rather a fulfilment of them. His Kingdom is one where a human being really is doing a great job of subduing and reigning and multiplying blessing through people. The kind of rule that was lost in the garden is now fully regained by Jesus, who fits perfectly into the patterns and prophecies, the yearning and longings, the templates and strategies of the Old Testament. And where these were dreams, or at best limited realities in those days, Jesus really does live the man-ruling-on-earth-with-God life consistently and with integrity. To those of us who know there's a gap between how we would like ourselves and our world to be and how it actually is, then this bridge-building example of paradise possibilities is very good news.

God Spelled Jesus

The word 'gospel' evokes all kinds of meanings and ideas. It is the name given to the four stories about Jesus as extended messages of 'good news' – which is what the word gospel literally means. Within the church, the gospel is often interpreted as the good news that there is forgiveness and new life. It is a 'spiritual' reality that transcends earthly life and gives a hope that whatever corruption there is in the here and now, those who receive this good message will have a new existence beyond even death. Jesus certainly emphasised an inner life of heart and behavioural purity alongside his dealing with immediate external realities of sickness and injustice. The shortness of his earthly ministry and the stories of his death, resurrection and ascension further accentuate this focus on the spiritual causes of sin, sickness and death and then victory over them. Jesus also talks of a spiritual contest and the power of evil and increasingly in his teaching he mentions the end times and a life that continues beyond this one.

This new afterlife is also explored brilliantly and much more fully by St Paul in his letters and has become what most people think the Christian message is all about. It is then expressed in cultural forms such as music, church revivals, gentle children's evangelists and angry street corner sermonizers.

Jesus was proclaiming the gospel, however, well before he mentions his death and resurrection. How can this be, if these are the events that define the spiritual reality that we call the gospel?

Jesus went throughout Galilee, teaching in their synagogues, proclaiming the good news of the kingdom, and healing every disease and illness among the people.[107]

Now after John had been taken into custody, Jesus came into Galilee, preaching the gospel of God, and saying, "The time is fulfilled, and the kingdom of God is at hand; repent and believe in the gospel."[108]

While the sun was setting, all those who had any who were sick with various diseases brought them to Him; and laying His hands on each one of them, He was healing them. Demons also were coming out of many, shouting, "You are the Son of God!" But rebuking them, He would not allow them to speak, because they knew Him to be the Christ.

When day came, Jesus left and went to a secluded place; and the crowds were searching for Him, and came to Him and tried to keep Him from going away from them. But He said to them, "I must preach the kingdom of God to the other cities also, for I was sent for this purpose."[109]

This is how three of the gospel writers describe the beginning of Jesus' ministry. In each account, the phrase 'good news' or 'gospel' is linked with the phrase 'Kingdom of God' or 'Kingdom of Heaven'. Not only does Jesus proclaim this good news of a new Kingdom arriving on earth, but his announcement is done in deeds as well as words as every kind of sickness and disease is healed.

107. Matthew 4:23.
108. Mark 1:14-15.
109. Luke 4:40-43.

The good news that Jesus proclaims here is immediate and effective. People's lives are actually changed and where they are tormented by sickness and evil, they are set free. The Kingdom that Jesus is heralding is the same as was spoken about by the prophets in their vision of a Jubilee world.

Although the phrase 'Gospel of the Kingdom' is gradually shortened to 'the gospel' as the gospel accounts progress and also in the New Testament letters, it is none the less a gospel *of* something rather than just a noun summing up the spiritual aspect of Jesus' mission. The gospel is often the Gospel of the Kingdom of God or of heaven, the gospel of God, the gospel of peace, the gospel of Jesus Christ/His Son, the gospel of grace, the gospel of salvation.[110]

As the good news of the Kingdom is announced it is a formal announcement that there is a new King. Typically in Roman times a gospel announcement would declare the reign of the Emperor and emphasise his qualities and victories. The stone of Priene, now in Izmir museum, was found with an inscription from 9BC that celebrates the birthday of Caesar Augustus:

> *It seemed good to the Greeks of Asia, in the opinion of the high priest Apollonius of Menophilus Azanitus: 'Since Providence, which has ordered all things and is deeply interested in our life, has set in most perfect order by giving us Augustus, whom she filled with virtue that he might benefit humankind, sending him as a saviour, both for us and for our descendants,*

---

110. Luke 16:16; Mark 1:1; Ephesians 6:16; Acts 20:24. There are numerous other references to the gospel covering all these meanings throughout.

that he might end war and arrange all things, and since he, Caesar, by his appearance (excelled even our anticipations), surpassing all previous benefactors, and not even leaving to posterity any hope of surpassing what he has done, and since the birthday of the god Augustus was the beginning of the good tidings for the world that came by reason of him],' which Asia resolved in Smyrna . . ."[111]

It is not surprising, then that the announcement of the birth of Jesus is made in similar style a few years later:

But the angel said to them, "Do not be afraid; for behold, I bring you good news of great joy which will be for all the people; for today in the city of David there has been born for you a Saviour, who is Christ the Lord.[112]

Josephus, the first century Jewish historian, writes that Tiberius read aloud the 'good news' declaration that Vespasian has been declared Emperor in the East.[113] He then continues, "good news from Rome . . . The whole empire being now secured and the Roman state saved beyond expectation".[114] It was typical for a Roman military leader to have been dignified with a 'Triumph' where he would have been honoured by leading a parade of captives into Rome. 'Good News' was also a well-known concept in the ancient Greek world. The 'gospel' occurs many times in Aeschylus' tragedy *Agamemnon*, the first part of the Oresteia, where the good news about the victory of the Greeks over Troy is

---

111. Evans, Craig A. "Mark's Incipit and Priene Calendar Inscription: From Jewish Gospel to Greco-Roman Gospel." *Journal of Greco-Roman Christianity and Judaism*, 67-81, 2000. Emphasis added.
112. Luke 2:10-11.
113. Flavius, Josephus and William Whiston. *The Genuine Works of Flavius Josephus, the Jewish Historian*. South Carolina: Nabu Press, 2012.
114. Ibid.

announced with excitement and in detail by messengers. If you have a spare 12 hours, do watch this this play, preferably in the baking heat of an original Greek auditorium so that the real meaning of Good News – i.e. the end of the play and bedtime – will become apparent.

This kind of announcing of a new kind of rule, by Agamemnon, Vespasian or any new king, is not that different to the kind of announcing that would have happened at the year of Jubilee. A jubal horn would be blown to declare that the time at last had arrived for the Jubilee celebration of a new way of doing things to begin. So when, in Luke 4, Jesus stands up in the synagogue and tells everyone that the beginning of the year of God's favour, the year of Jubilee, has now arrived (because the signs of it are being fulfilled through Him), it is as if he is blowing the trumpet to announce this new reality. And as he goes about the towns and villages in Roman-occupied Judea, he is announcing that a new king has been born in the East and he is leading a train of released captives in his wake.[115]

Selah, pause, reflect

New eternal life, free from sin and pain and death, is the most wonderful promise. What does this look like if it starts now and not just when we physically die?

How does spiritual freedom affect earthly freedom? What are the linkages between these two freedoms in your own life and experience?

---

115. Matthew 2:2, Ephesians 4:8.

A new spirituality:
The Kingdom is a culture and ethos

So, we see that the 'gospel' is the good news about the Kingdom of Heaven, and it begins its new rule in Jesus as he cares for people, overturns their sicknesses and the effects of their circumstances, and begins to subdue the corruption and bitterness that is on the earth and in the cosmos through his power-filled love. It is not limited to personal piety or expressed only in religious devotion, any more than Adam and Eve were only told to hold church services and prayer vigils. The Kingdom of Heaven as expressed by Jesus is about restoring a way of living for the planet and its people that actually works well and is no longer obstructed by sickness, poverty, selfishness, violence or even death.

What is fascinating is how Jesus looks more deeply into the heart of man rather than simply running a health service, following a political model or establishing a set of rules for a new society. His healings and works of justice and restoration are definitely what the Kingdom is about, but it seems he can only effect this as someone who is not caught up with the struggles of Cain or the frustration of Lamech or the thousand and one reasons any of us have to betray our desire for Shalom. As a new emperor, with lots of obvious power, he could have arrived doing the miracles he did and then insisted that we all go along with it: a kind of forced utopia. What he does instead, though, is reveal that where in the past cities and communities have been modelled prophetically by God's messengers, they have only ever worked when those who are at the grassroots level have a change of heart and mind.

In this way, there is an internal dimension to the Kingdom. It really is about our 'spirituality'. In fact, it is exactly our spirituality that Jesus defines for humanity. The whole point of creation was for the heavens and the earth to be joined and for God to dwell with mankind on the earth as people invite him into the fruitfully cultivated dominion. But as people ended up estranged from God, so their spiritual lives and earthly lives became disjointed. So, it is not a surprise that in our search for a transcendent God and His Kingdom, we tend to ignore the state of the earth and instead put our hope in the beyond. Nor is it a surprise that we don't often look for Him or acknowledge His interest in our daily life. As Jesus brings the Kingdom of Heaven with him to earth, he once more brings the heavens and the earth into contact. And this is not a once a week religious event in a special place, but it is in a sick mother-in-law's bedroom, on a Saturday rambler's association walk through the wheat fields and in a crowded home where he is desperately hungry even for a pot noodle.[116]

Jesus redefines spirituality as being our everyday lives shot through with the nature of God's love and peace. Just as the Kingdom of Heaven is expressed in subduing electricity and drinking a flat white, so it is also expressed in love, joy and peace experienced in, and pouring out of, our hearts. Jesus managed to combine all these territories – of heart, body, relationships and earth – in his good news of the Kingdom. His Kingdom of Heaven is truly heavenly and truly earthly.

116. Mark 1:30, 2:23, 3:20.

It is spiritual in that it is all about the Breath-Spirit of God once more animating the rhythms of creation. It is natural in that this is the habitat in which God has chosen to live and rule. In fact, the Kingdom of Heaven can impact and bless anyone but, in order to multiply, will only really take more permanent root where there is a thirst and hunger for things to be set right.

The way to see the Kingdom of Heaven truly rule on the earth is for the hearts of men and women to also have this reign within them. The good news is that even hearts and minds can be changed. The Kingdom that Jesus proclaims is as much about attitudes, behaviours and the pre-eminence of love as it is about the activity of ruling and reigning. The Kingdom of Heaven is a culture and not a far off place, and the behaviours that are expressed in this culture are those of creativity and multiplication, service and protection. This is what was first intended – to cultivate the qualities of God within creation and see them spread. And then, similarly through the family and family of families, a culture both taught and caught would become the set of natural traits and espoused values of all those in its neighbourhood. Even in the Kingdom of Israel, it was not necessarily living in the geographical place that was important, but the culture of joyful obedience and a heart after God that could then be adopted by any nation around.

Jesus taught a new 'ethos', a Greek word that essentially means character. The Oxford English Dictionary definition of this is "the characteristic spirit of a people, community, culture, or era as manifested in its attitudes and aspirations".[117] A culture is how this spirit, or set of values,

---

117. "ethos, n.". OED Online. December 2019. Oxford University Press. https://www-oed-com. proxy.cc.uic.edu/view/Entry/64840?redirectedFrom=ethos (accessed February 10, 2020).

is patterned and repeated through behaviour and then transmitted through symbols, artifacts, achievements and language. Erwin McManus puts it this way in *An Unstoppable Force*: "Ethos – the fundamental character or spirit of a culture, the underlying sentiment that informs beliefs, customs, and practices of a community, group or person. To simplify an ethos is expressed through spontaneous recurring patterns."[118]

The ethos of this new Kingdom is essentially one of sacrificial love. The idea is that this then informs how we exercise those God-given impulses to subdue and rule, to serve and protect through recurring patterns that are spontaneous rather than forced. Jesus is the architect of a new culture. As the wise King, he knows that the Kingdom plan of Shalom will not work through command and control. Things might get done efficiently in this way, but they won't lead to life in all its fullness. Instead, there is the need for a new breath of life to make hearts beat in a fresh way, or a new language of ethos that is written into soft hearts rather than inscribed in a hard statute book. This was also prophesied, along with the vision for a Shalom Kingdom, in the Old Testament:

> *"I will put My law within them and on their heart I will write it; and I will be their God, and they shall be My people."*[119]

> *"Moreover, I will give you a new heart and put a new spirit within you; and I will remove the heart of stone from your flesh and give you a heart of flesh. I will put My Spirit within you and cause you to walk*

118. McManus, Erwin Raphael. *An Unstoppable Force: Daring to Become the Church God Had in Mind*. Colorado: David C Cook Publishing Company, 2013.
119. Jeremiah 31.

*in My statutes, and you will be careful to observe My
ordinances. You will live in the land that I gave to your
forefathers; so you will be My people, and I will be
your God."*[120]

The Kingdom of Heaven is expressed in the attitudes
and behaviour of people whose hearts are in line with
God's heart. In Jesus' most famous teaching, The Sermon
on the Mount, he describes what this culture looks like
when people are naturally seeking justice, peace and
joy.[121] The poor in spirit, those who mourn, the gentle,
the hungry for justice, the merciful, the pure in heart, the
peacemakers and those persecuted for righteousness: are
all described by Jesus as being joyfully content. Jesus often
describes people in this way: the English word 'blessed' or
'happy' is our translation. It is not a happiness to do with
circumstances or luck, nor a feeling that comes and goes,
rather this is the place of Shalom where people are deeply
content, delighted and surprised by joy.

The Kingdom of Heaven is a 'Way': a way of life; a way of
being; a mindset; an ethos. So, when Jesus announces
that the Kingdom of Heaven has arrived, he makes it clear
that although its rule can be felt by those in the vicinity, its
benefits are fully received through a total change of mind
or a new perspective. That would be the same for a newly
arrived visitor to any kingdom. The laws and habits would
apply and very probably affect this visitor quite deeply but
not turn them into a citizen. In the United Kingdom, there
would be the smell of fish and chips in the early evening, or

---

120. Ezekiel 36.
121. Matthew 5-7.

the proliferation of average speed cameras, the abundance of recycling bins and the no smoking in public places. These can be ignored – leading to a possible prosecution – or submitted to and even somewhat enjoyed, but it takes a shift in mentality to naturally obey, appreciate and even propagate the values behind them.

Jesus said repent and believe the good news.[122] That is: change the way you see yourself, the world and your place in it. Change your view of what you do and how you do it. Open your eyes to see heaven on earth. Turn away from the old laws of tit for tat, self protection and self promotion. The Kingdom is here and the joy of Plan A is back on!

The challenge is to believe this, to settle the weight of your confidence and shift your balance so your soul's fulcrum is now resting on the good news of the Kingdom of Heaven. The good news is that you don't need to defend yourself or promote yourself; there is a significance to who you are, what you do and how you do it. Heaven is not a ticketed far-off executive lounge for religious people, but very much part of what happens now.

Jesus announces this new Kingdom and also has a manifesto. He demonstrates what it is like in the here and now with healings, kindness, justice and courage. But he also begins to articulate how men and women might become citizens of this new Kingdom culture through discovering its ethos and then finding that, quite naturally, they are living and even spreading its benefits. What is strange and exciting is that this kind of living and reigning

122. Mark 1:15.

is done with order and planning – as we saw in the creation of the cosmos in Genesis 1 – but also with the crazy kind of multiplication and fruitfulness seen on an earth that is colourful, varied, and creative.

Dee Hock, former CEO of VISA, calls this kind of governance 'chaordic' and writes: "Purpose and principles clearly understood and articulated and commonly shared, are the genetic code of any healthy organisation. To the degree that you hold purpose and principles in common among you, you can dispense with command and control, people will know how to behave in accordance with them, and they'll do it in thousands of unimaginable and creative ways."[123]

Jesus' manifesto clearly articulated in Luke 4 when he reiterates Isaiah's Kingdom vision of a culture of peace. Shalom is in view: good news for the poor, release for captives, sight to blind, setting free the oppressed, and the year of God's favour. Just like the words spoken in the beginning that had power to make things happen and establish multiplication and fruitfulness, so these words are not simply what Jesus himself would do, but they are the what will happen in thousands of unimaginable and creative ways through those who commonly share, articulate and understand the Kingdom's purpose and principles.

---

123. Hock, Dee. *Birth of the Chaordic Age*. San Francisco: Berrett-Koehler Publishers, 1999.

Selah, pause, reflect

The teaching of Jesus is often a description of a new reality rather than a set of rules to abide by.
What behaviours stem naturally from your heart that are good? How did that happen?

How has the experience of prayer, encounter and knowing God's word fashioned such values in your heart and mind?

Is there a value of Jesus that you would like to live by and have naturally in your character? Talk to God about it and begin to fix your thoughts on this. See what happens when you prayerfully let this quality grow in you over the next few weeks.

Kingdom Culture:
a culture of cultures,
just like a family of families

A new Kingdom of Heaven culture serves rather than oppresses the earth. When a new kingdom rises within or outside of other existing kingdoms, what often takes place is a usurping, or a bulldozing, or supplanting. This can be an act of extreme violence; it may include degradation and eroding of language, history and national identity. The arrival of the Kingdom of Heaven has a struggle: there is a resistance to its culture of Shalom, which looks like war. Nevertheless, it is not a Kingdom that sets up a new cultural ethos by squashing the existing cultural identities. It is a Kingdom not of this world. In the Kingdom of Heaven will be every tribe, nation and tongue: cultural identities intact. What Jesus came to bring was freedom from the aspects of our existing cultures that oppress and destroy.

In our zeal, we like to think that we know what these more cancerous aspects of anti-Kingdom culture are. Some may be obviously counter to Jesus' Kingdom – the culture of slavery, the oppression of women and the exploitation of children. Jesus demonstrated that his new Kingdom was quite different to the kingdoms of his time with regard to these things. Nevertheless, we have a habit of thinking – traced back to that tree of the knowledge of good and evil once again – that we can judge what is in and what is out: what aspects of earthly culture contribute to the wealth of a new Jerusalem and what aspects need to be prevented from being brought into the city.

One thing is sure, the Kingdom of Heaven is characterised by men and women from different nationalities, backgrounds, culture and subcultures, who all share a new Father, a new DNA. It is at its richest when cultural divides are crossed – especially those that historically have been deeply antagonistic. As tribes and nations, we have found differing ways of fulfilling the command to subdue. Our forming and our fashioning are all in the image of God but come from different angles and perspectives. Our fruitfulness is displayed in physical appearance, language, clothing, cuisine, music and humour. In fact, such an array of difference, which then joins with the differences of the rest of non-human creation, is what makes the Kingdom of Heaven so marvellous and wild. It is stretched to what seems breaking point, only to reveal new dimensions of hues, fragrance and flavour.

Jesus said that the good news of the Kingdom should be proclaimed to all nations or people groups, and disciples and Kingdom apprentices found in each of these groups.[124] The first major church outside of Israel is listed as having leaders who were different in skin colour, ethnicity, social background, and citizenship.[125] Talking of the antagonism between Jews and gentiles, Paul writes:

And He came and preached peace to you who were far away, and peace to those who were near; for through Him we both have our access in one Spirit to the Father. So then you are no longer strangers and aliens, but you are fellow citizens with the saints, and are of God's household, having been built on the foundation of the

124. Matthew 28:18-20, Matthew 90, Acts 13:1.
125. Acts 13:1.

apostles and prophets, Christ Jesus Himself being the corner stone, in whom the whole building, being fitted together, is growing into a holy temple in the Lord, in whom you also are being built together into a dwelling of God in the Spirit.[126]

There is one big family, made up of lots of families, and one family home where the pans are on the stove, the pots are in the oven and the meal that we will share with one another will be distinctly 'ethnic'. The fact that the Kingdom of Heaven brings together and completes those things that, till now, have not fitted well together, is its beauty and strength. The feast of nations will not be a single dominant dish, nor a fair, but utilitarian rotor of recipes. It will require that humanity be at its most creative and servant-hearted; a combination of skill and riotous abandon; chaordism (if that's a word now) at its multiculoured multi languaged best.

Kingdom Culture: Inversion, Subversion, Conversion

If the Kingdom has its own culture, in what ways is that different to the cultures we know and understand already? It is certainly a culture where fruitfulness and generosity and overflow are significant. It is also characterised by the Shalom features of Jesus' manifesto, as well as those others from Isaiah that include all kinds of freedoms and inclusion for those whose lives, bodies and circumstances have meant they are often pushed out on to the edge of community life. The properties of the paradise garden are there in the Kingdom culture – the importance of creative pressure and good rule; the serving and the protecting of

---

126. Ephesians 2:17-22.

what is entrusted. In the beginning of creation, it is evident that in God himself is the pre-eminent value of love, as He appears as Father and Son and Spirit, where somehow within himself he is able to prefer and esteem, delight in and be delighted by. So, too, the culture of the Kingdom is about relationships and community and family, or as the Bible often puts it, tribe, nation and tongue.

Therefore, the Kingdom of Heaven's culture is radically different to the culture of other empires and kingdoms we are used to. These go all the way back to Cain's and Lamech's desire for revenge, a culture not simply of an eye for an eye, tooth for a tooth; but a life for an eye, or the death of a child for a tooth. In fact, the cultures that surround the first chosen family are exactly like this in character, and the individuals in that family and then in the growing people of Israel family find it hard to act any differently. Samson, a judge favoured by God, loses his temper in ways that escalate pain. King Saul is suspicious and dreads David for being congratulated by women. There is slaughter and mayhem all around. The empire that Jesus is born into is no paradise garden. After exhibiting some strong values as a republic, Rome has grown sick and cruel. As Hamlet would say, "It is an unweeded garden. Things gross and rank in nature possess it merely."[127]

In fact, some of the most well known aspects today of Jesus' teaching are his summings-up of a heavenly culture that is so different it surely cannot work. It looks weakly wishful. It undermines what we hold dear and is rash foolishness for anyone who tries to put it into practice. It has been said

t, Act 1, Scene 2.

many times that the Kingdom of Heaven is an upside down kingdom. As such, it is either laughably fragile or strongly subversive.

This is also the nature of comedy. Those in power lose it. New clothes and identities are exchanged. In English tradition, there is a celebration called the Feast of Fools. This is when the Lord of Misrule causes the servants to rule over the kings. It is quite similar to Saturnalia, the Roman tradition of this inversion of power. This is the heart of comedy and it is not surprising that it is found in cultural traditions throughout history. There are even parallels with Roman tradition to hail a new boy king for a short period of time who will then be sacrificed. This is what happened in the dark and evil 'comedy' of Jesus' mocking torture and death. But in life, the quirky, alluring, wrong-but-so-right Kingdom that Jesus preached has a power that cannot be snuffed out.

Kingdom Culture: Divine Comedy

The words and parables of Jesus are filled with ironic, comic, Lord of Misrule situations:

The blesseds of the beatitudes are ironic and bizarre.[128] Most of these predicaments are reasons to weep and give up.

The first shall be last and the last shall be first.[129] And what about those who have worked jolly hard to be first, or those who were born first and have done a good job, or

---

128. Matthew 5:1-12 - the poor in spirit are blessed.
129. Matthew 20:16 - the last shall be first.

those who are last, because, quite frankly, we think they deserve to be?

The youngest and the poorest and sickest attract the king's love and friendship more than the cool, attractive, clever and deserving.[130] The gospels of Jesus are littered with stories of Jesus stopping to talk to the wrong people and letting down the kind of people he really needs on side. It appears impolite and at times a waste of the limited resources of time, energy and, dare we say, power that Jesus has.

Even those who have worked very hard, in fact slaved to be good for God, somehow find themselves outside of the party.[131] This is from a story Jesus tells of two brothers and their father. It is annoying because the one who seems to be like me and has stuck pretty close to the God-like figure misses out – and has always missed out, it seems – on the fun.

If you have given yourself to what you think is good and right, you may end up with no more reward than someone who very late in the day has hung on to your coat tails and freeloaded on your effort.[132] Another frustrating story about a God figure who values his kindness over his apparent fairness. (Although to be truly fair, he didn't actually break his word, the characters should have just been a bit more canny in their negotiating with him.)

---

130. Luke 8:44 - Jesus lets his mission to the official be interrupted by the poorest woman.
131. Luke 15:11-32 - the profligate son gets a party; the hardworking son feels overlooked.
132. Matthew 20:1-16 - the workers employed last get paid as much as those who've worked all day.

It is more satisfying to give than to receive.[133] A provocative phrase of Jesus that seems to sum it all up. I really like receiving because it makes me feel valued at last. It is hard that someone else feels more valued than me when they serve me.

It is hard to be wealthy.[134] There's one bloke who actually seems pretty keen on Jesus and the Kingdom, and has even got some resources that could spread the Kingdom well. And he isn't encouraged as much as I think he should be. Jesus doesn't go running after him to make things better.

Serving enemies is seen as a good thing.[135] Whether this is a Roman soldier or a woman who appears to have been faithless, is sectarian and not even her villagers appear to like her, or whether it is people who actually are hurting you with such hatred and zeal, surely this niceness will just lead to people taking advantage.

And as for forgiveness and grace – even the Bible declares this as scandalous.
It is all upside down.[136] For most of us who have a conscience and a strong set of values this overly gracious kingdom feels annoying, and for those who haven't given it – or anyone else for that matter – much thought or attention, it is great news. Surely life should be easier if you have wealth. There should be more rewards for doing stuff right. It is sensible to hold back on grace in order to not be taken advantage of . . .

---

133. Acts 20:35 - it is more blessed to give than receive.
134. Matthew 19:16-26 - the rich young ruler who has lived according to the law is challenged to give his wealth away, too.
135. John 4:1-43 - the Samaritan woman has VIP access to Jesus the rabbi.
136. 1 Corinthians 1:23 - Jesus is a stumbling block and foolishness to some.

There is a huge tension in how we experience the culture of the Kingdom. On the one hand, our God-given human DNA knows it is right – we flourish and multiply as we pursue the inbuilt attributes to create, build and fashion, and to relate, be fruitful and multiply. On the other hand, where this is corrupted, it clashes with the Kingdom culture of service, of protecting others and above all, of sacrificial love. We embrace the Kingdom and we reject the Kingdom. All at once. There are times when it is hard to see where our good experience becomes corrupted and our bad experience ends up finding grace.

Nevertheless, when we look at the person of Jesus, he is very impressive. His is a modelled life that is actually quite heroic and mesmerisingly attractive for men and women. Not only that, the people around him who begin to change in heart and mind also take on these qualities and live a life of freedom despite the external pressures on them. History then tells of this movement gathering pace, and despite the same hiccups seen in Gideon, Samson, Saul and David, there is enough fragrance of the Kingdom filling the world in small and also quite significant ways, to make us sit up and wonder if actually it really does have a pervasive and subversive strength.

Kingdom Culture: Surprise, surprise

As the clouds of the Kingdom come near and drop their dew, the new air that is breathed is quite intoxicating:

Free from the sour breath of bitterness. To not be caught up in choking angry resentment through mistreatment and abuse is a wonderful thing. It is bad enough to be oppressed from people outside of us, then to also find an inner oppression of anger, bitterness and stomach churning sickness.

Not choked by poverty spirited greed. To be free of the constant drive to gain wealth for power's sake means there are actually more options for how we use our skills and talents. In fact, the promise of the Kingdom that we can receive all we are looking for, for free, rather than by accumulating wealth is a gift! Wanting to win the lottery is a fair enough dream, because we are searching for rest, freedom from anxiety, some great holidays and the chance to handle beautiful things. This looks a lot like Shalom and the paradise garden commission. To imagine that we can live in the peace of what such money buys, without having to have and spend that money is a wild and wonderful thought. And then to be able to handle finance freely and generously without our inner Gollum wheezing 'My Precious" – this is the subversive Kingdom of Heaven.

The surprising tastes and touches of things being set right that were wrong. Whether it is a physical disease, a relationship breakdown, or a broken heart – solutions are often beyond us in the here and now. The Kingdom of Heaven is where the restoration in these things is in evidence. Around Jesus the King they began to break in, signs of a way of being that had been far off but now is very much closer. Rectifying, redeeming, restoring are all great kingdom verbs – Look, I am making all things new! Before our very eyes!

Courage. To face disaster and meanness and violence, holding five small stones when faced with a giant warrior, is evidence of the Kingdom. The fact that such courageous love has a way of combating and even winning over the giants is extraordinary. How can it be that armies or political systems are felled with seed-like faith actions? – whether it is Rosa Parkes sitting firm on her seat on a bus, or Martin Luther nailing his convictions to the Wittenberg door.

The utter relief of being forgiven. The reassurance of not having to be defensive or be weighed low by the catalogue of mistakes and hurts we have left behind in our wake, is the song of Kingdom freedom. That this kind of setting free then inevitably pays forward is wonderful. In a reflection of the Kingdom nature of things multiplying after their own kind, so, the grace-power of one freed slave leads to many others being forgiven and sent on their way. This is probably why people will go and see "Les Miserables" many times. If the Kingdom of Heaven is like that (and set to music), we'd like to be in.

No longer at the mercy of bad luck, misfortune, or unseen forces. There's even a subversive power that goes beyond the earthly and natural. As we read in Genesis 1 there are earthly realms and heavenly realms, and where the heavenly realms are also in rebellion to the King, then it seems we are at the mercy of gods over which we have no control or influence. We may call this fate, or luck. We may call them demons and demi gods. In the beginning, Adam and Eve had authority on the earth over everything that went on here, including the unseen unknown powers and angels. But then the utter chaos of those pre-history days on the earth where "all our thoughts were only evil" revealed that this was no longer the case. But in Jesus there is a definite declaration of war and strong authority exercised even over those forces that grip us, or brood over peoples and places. How subversive that in Mark 4 the storm of the waters (often an image for spiritual heavenly rebellion in the Bible) is calmed by a few words from a still yawning hair tousled Jesus. And how remarkable and stunning that people and places so obviously possessed or overrun with hatred and evil are emptied of such filth and clothed and in their right mind once more.[137]

The Kingdom of Heaven, for all its perceived weakness, pastel shaded gentleness and insipid kindness, has a power that stands strong before even the mightiest empire.

Selah, pause, reflect

Kumar's story:

I am from a Dalit background, constantly hearing from my mother that we are untouchables and subhuman in my childhood days!

I faced constant discrimination and dehumanisation in my school days. Remembering when I was around 11 years old, playing cricket against the upper caste boys, during which I accidentally bumped into an upper caste boy who yelled at me, shouting, "You dirty Dalit dog!" Hearing this derogatory term, I was angry and hit him with my cricket bat. He was hurt and was bleeding.

---

137. Luke 8:22-39.

Within no time, around 50 to 60 of his upper caste friends and relatives arrived and declared that I deserved a punishment, which was to vacate the village in 24 hours' time! We were shattered and did the same, otherwise they would have hurt us physically. we relocated to another village.

That was the time I went into a life depression and isolation in my teenage years. Being fed up of viewed as worthless human, I wanted to end my life.

One day, my elder brother came and shared that he accepted Christ and pointed out an amazing statement from the Bible: "I am created in the IMAGE OF GOD!"

I instantly grabbed the Gospel and received Christ!

Kumar is now a bishop in Good Shepherd Church India, a new Anglican style denomination with over four thousand churches, with schools and economic, health and anti-trafficking projects. Christian Bishops have recognised status in the modern Indian constitution.

Kingdom vs. Empire

Jesus and Caesar – which truth is the evangelion?

Jesus doesn't talk about Himself as King very often – he simply acts as the King and talks about the Kingdom. It is clear that where the Kingdom is, so he is exercising its rule; therefore, he is the King. But he does call himself the King, ironically and bravely, to Pontius Pilate, who represents the world's king at that time, the Emperor Caesar Augustus. Most of Jesus' time has been spent with people on the margins and he has made it clear that the Kingdom of Heaven is for these people and not yet another club for the powerful. But just before he is killed, Jesus confronts the world power of the Roman Empire. In this, he demonstrates that there is a big difference between the Kingdom of Heaven and the nature of empire.

The word 'empire' comes from the word command – where things get done through the command of forceful power. This is how we would usually assume we get our will done. The more force we have, the more likely it is that what we want will happen.

We also attribute this characteristic to God. Because He is God and therefore all-powerful, then this must be his final default mode. We assume that although he is loving, at the end of the day as God, he'll clear up using force. Jesus the King doesn't do this at the end of His day. He keeps on loving. And if he is the King and the image of the invisible God, then we can assume that God is not actually this vengeful hero after all.

Therefore Pilate entered again into the Praetorium, and summoned Jesus and said to Him, "Are You the King of the Jews?" Jesus answered, "Are you saying this on your own initiative, or did others tell you about Me?" Pilate answered, "I am not a Jew, am I? Your own nation and the chief priests delivered You to me; what have You done?" Jesus answered, "My kingdom is not of this world. If My kingdom were of this world, then My servants would be fighting so that I would not be handed over to the Jews; but as it is, My kingdom is not of this realm." Therefore Pilate said to Him, "So You are a king?" Jesus answered, "You say correctly that I am a king. For this I have been born, and for this I have come into the world, to testify to the truth. Everyone who is of the truth hears My voice." Pilate said to Him, "What is truth?"[138]

When Jesus is brought in front of Pilate for trial, it is actually Jesus who is doing the confronting. He reveals the truth: that the empire's strength is in the fact that those who are part of it must serve the empire to serve themselves. Pilate could at this moment have spoken for himself, but his drive for security and significance means he doesn't speak on his own initiative. Jesus' power is not an empire command power. He simply states what is true and raises the confrontation to a whole new level by talking about His Kingdom.

The phrase 'not of this world' does not mean it is only ethereal or spiritual. It has been demonstrated that it really is a kingdom for and of both earth and heaven. But it does

138. John 18:33-38.

not have the same ethos as the world currently does. It is not built on the same foundations of self-serving and self-protection. Jesus declares that if His Kingdom was of the world, then it would resort to the usual route of sheer might and Jesus could have easily escaped. Even Satan knew this in that similar confrontation in the wilderness.[139] He knew that Jesus could be rescued by a heavenly power at any time. He also knew that Jesus, as co-creator, could intervene into creation at any point and turn it to his personal advantage, as stones becoming bread on his whim. Like Pilate, Satan showed Jesus the kingdoms of the world and had his own power to offer a 'freedom' within these.

Pilate is left with no option, as a man of empire. If Jesus is King, as he says he is, then he needs to be killed because the other prisoner, Barabbas (who is of this world), if freed, can easily be stamped out later by a bigger, stronger jackboot. Jesus makes his declaration that he was born for this: born to be King, King of this kind of Shalom Kingdom, which means ironically being born to die at the hands of such an enemy. He was born to testify to this truth: that even the violence of the empire's death-making cannot in the end prevent abundant life from flourishing and being fruitful.

In Matthew's account, there is a brief verse just before Jesus is sentenced. While Pilate is in the judgement seat, his wife sends him a message that she had a disturbing dream about Jesus and knows him to be righteous. Even at moments when storms are raging, for those like her whose imaginations are open to new perception, a new belief begins because the Kingdom comes close. Perhaps

---

139. Matthew 4:1-11.

we all sometimes wonder at what we do see, in glimpses of breathtaking clarity, but then ignore what we don't want to see, even if it is staring us in the face.

So, Pilate's final question could be a sneer or could be his own final retort that the challenge at Jesus' death is the contest between the empire of this world and the Kingdom of Heaven. Which rule is really true? Which rule actually works and will continue to work? Is the power of sacrificial love stronger than the power of getting what you want done?

Jesus goes meekly like a lamb to the slaughter. He then rises on the first day of the new week in a garden where everything has started to become new.

Violence, pressure and conflict

This encounter between Jesus and Pilate is intensely dramatic but not as violently theatrical as the stoning of Stephen or the sicknesses of Job. Nevertheless, for Jesus to proclaim that he is King of a Kingdom of love and grace does not mean that this new culture is established just by the growing of daffodils, or welcomed with open arms by chieftains and warlords the world over. The conflict looks calm between Pilate and Jesus but immediately becomes bloodied and violent. Pilate is able to wash this filth off his hands, but the scars remain on Jesus' own.

A satisfying drama is where a good and moral hero is under pressure but does not break. Nevertheless, it is often so pleasing when this same hero finally gets huge revenge on his or her enemy, preferably using that enemy's weapons against them. This is a myth that is parallel to the Kingdom, but the ultimate moment may appeal more to our deep-down desire for retribution than an honourable declaration of justice that rises in our spirit. Even the best of us would quite like an element of the Kingdom of Heaven to have some good old-fashioned revenge, or at least the haughty but nice satisfaction that you made the right choices and are sipping pina coladas while other, less savvy competitors are still in the pitstop changing their tyres or slowly collecting the final clues. How odd that even the calmest of us really want the hero to nail the baddie and wreak some horrible, violent revenge. And yet, when we see this rage bubbling up in a hero, knowing that it will lead to their own downfall, we desperately want to stop them.

Watching a film in a small cinema recently, a woman near the front broke all English conventions of audience non-participation by crying out "Don't do it!" when the hero grabbed a hold of his deceiving wife. I thought this mad lady was angrily shouting at him to leave the woman alone. At the end of the film, I realised the crazy crier was one of the friends with whom I had come to the cinema.[140] She was shouting at the character in order to protect him, to shield him from giving in to his wife's goading, rather than against his potential aggression towards her. How wretchedly confusing as we pull apart the pages of the book we are reading in the hope that the protagonist will either get revenge or resist taking revenge. What do we do with our pent up desire for judgement, justice and power, yet also our recognition that in the pursuit of this, Macbeth, Othello, and Brad Pitt could end up as bad as their rivals?

---

140. Due to a booking error I was not sitting near my friend in that cinema. This was a relief. The same error also led to my wife being given a tall dining chair to sit on in the second row in the absence of a soft, low theatre seat. This was embarrassing. It was an odd evening.

This is not to say that the end of the Kingdom v anti-Kingdom story is one of stalemate, or lack of (in the mediaeval sense) satisfaction. If Jesus the King ends up fighting with the same weapons we have always fought with, only more efficiently or with masterful skill, then His Kingdom is really no different from any empire where might is right and command controls. But Jesus, the lamb who was slain, standing by the throne (his humility means that you eventually only see him there after first being impressed by the four creatures and the twenty-four elders in Revelation 5), does not finally wield an AK-47. He continues to love with such a passion that anyone or thing that comes close most likely finds themselves in submission, gratefully cultivated and protected.

Frustratingly for us would-be revenge-revolutionaries, the power with which the Kingdom comes is the power of humility, sacrifice and love. This is opposed by the power of force and might. The result, though, is still violent and messy. There is still a clash and there are casualties. This is seen with clarity in the Book of Daniel and its Kingdom of Heaven perspective. Not only have we seen Daniel fulfil the mandate to rule and reign in a compromised world, Daniel himself is under immense pressure from the power of the empire, and he and his friends find themselves thrown violently into situations of fear and death. The visions and dreams are likewise violent, this time on an international and even cosmic scale, encompassing whole generations. The in-breaking of God's rule is effective and decisive in these examples: the rock that shatters the other Kingdom statue elements. Although the growth of the Kingdom is slow and strategic, and reliant on people with loving hearts who are willing to place themselves in the right place at the right time, we see too that the Kingdom of Heaven invades the earth with remarkable speed and power. When Jesus announces the arrival of the Kingdom, he is announcing a new rule and a culture of Shalom, but he is also declaring war on all that has corrupted God's plan for a great earth.

Kicking and Screaming

Jesus says that judgement is on the world (or literally cosmos) and that its current ruler, the accusing enemy, will be forcibly kicked out.[141] Such a pushing out is a phrase most often used of Jesus as he drives out demons and spiritual forces. Somehow, in a heavenly or 'spiritual' realm, the Kingdom comes with power and is opposed with power.

The Kingdom breaks out, breaks through, breaks upon or spreads out. In the Old Testament there is an ancestor of Jesus called Perez, or Breakthrough.[142] This word is often used when God decides to intervene, and heaven breaks into the earth in remarkable ways. In fact, the warrior King David calls God the God of the Breakthrough.[143] This is what it means to be praying for the Kingdom of Heaven to come on the earth, for what happens in heaven to happen here, as Jesus taught his disciples to pray. In these times, our usual half-hearted casual ignorance is not enough to handle the current of the Kingdom, but when we pray, the breaking through of heaven comes like a torrent to breach the walls of oppression and fear.

Often, we use the word breakthrough where there is some kind of scientific discovery, like a medical breakthrough,

---

141. John 12:31.
142. Genesis 39. Perez breaks through at birth and saves the lives of his twin brother, Zerah and mother because of the impending life-threatening shoulder presentation of Zerah. See its associated verb, too, as descendants spread out in Genesis 28.
143. 2 Samuel 5:20.

where such a discovery enables death and disease to be thwarted. It is what happens when a tunnel is finally completed. On 1 December 1990, Graham Fagg of Great Britain and Philippe Cozette of France broke through the final inches of rock, 130 feet below sea level, to complete three years digging of the channel railway tunnel between Dover and Calais. A military breakthrough changes the nature of a war. The end of American Civil War is attributed to a battle called the Breakthrough of Petersburgh on April 2 1865.

In all these examples there is resistance, against which is brought a determined concentration of power. This is the same kind of fierce determination Jesus carried in his strongly meek encounter with Pilate. The Kingdom is not about weak, blancmange-spirited yes-men. Proverbs 25 says, "*Like* a city that is broken into *and* without walls is a man who has no control over his spirit."[144]

My school winter rugby-playing days were characterised by the fact that I could run fast and so ended up on the wing. This meant that I happily but shiveringly avoided any action and could daydream unhindered. But if, by any wished-against fluke, the ball did get to me, I made sure that I ran away rather than concentrated my 'power' on breaking through the stockier, heavier opposition. I disappointed the teacher. It is actually more Christlike to set your face like flint towards your goal and break others free in your pursuit of victory.

It is this same wall-breaking Perez power that is also referred to in the Bible as 'overflow'. For instance, this is the characteristic of the Kingdom where there is more than

---

144. Emphasis original.

enough wine in the vats.[145] The Perez fruitfulness of God-blessed humanity will spread out.[146] A breaking through happens because goodness is so good and so full that when the Kingdom arrives, the collision is a result of it fulfilling its natural inclination towards being fruitful and overflowing. It breaks through walls and anti-Kingdom defences. To be fruitful and to multiply is the inherent power of God's rule. It happens in the days of creation and is the command-gift of God to mankind. It is no surprise, then, that when Jesus shouted out that he was a river of life and that such water would flow out of a believer's innermost being, he was very soon opposed and struck down.[147] It is this kind of baptism that the earth had seen before, where the spreading out of waters cleansed the whole land. Such a baptism of life and Shalom is the last thing an enemy to the Kingdom wants to experience. The bursting out of water and blood from Jesus' broken side is also the breaking through and the kicking out of all that is opposed to the kindness of God's rule.

Such an in-breaking or out-breaking is quite different from ideas of the Kingdom of Heaven growing gradually, or spreading quietly and unobtrusively throughout the world until everything gets nicer and nicer or life becomes better and better. We will see that the Kingdom is indeed quiet, and does indeed spread like yeast. It is small and seemingly insignificant, and its power is also subtly and humbly world-changing. This does not mean, however, that the breakthroughs never happened, or have stopped happening, or are in some way uncharacteristically ineffective.

---

145. Proverbs 3:10 (see also the same image but different vocabulary in the Pentecost Kingdom prophecy of Joel 2:24).
146. Job 1:10, Genesis 28:14, Isaiah 54:3.
147. John 7:37-53.

Jesus' proof that the Kingdom had arrived (and is still arriving) is given in his answer to John the Baptist's disciples. John was not in the vanguard of a new triumphant procession. Instead he was in prison, and soon to lose his head. It is not surprising that he was thinking that perhaps Jesus wasn't the King after all. His response is typical of any of us. If it's not happening to us, it's not happening – especially if we expect to have a ringside seat. (He is untypical of us in that he spotted the Kingdom before it had gone public, gave way to the King rather than establishing his own mini-empire, and then ended up in prison having bravely confronted a kingdom of this world in the shape of Herod's greed, lust and fascist collaboration.) Jesus replies by using the Isaiah Kingdom proofs: "The blind receive sight and the lame walk, the lepers are cleansed and the deaf hear, the dead are raised up, and the poor have the gospel preached to them."[148] (He misses out the freedom for prisoners, which would have been very good news for John to hear!) Jesus is saying that the Kingdom arrives and has immediate effects. Its power is able to reverse the corruption of sickness and selfishness. The reports of this are everywhere in Judea and even reach King Herod's palace. For John, in the middle of the battlefield, however, the Kingdom arrives with a call to trust and have faith while all around is chaos. Such a summing up of the activity of the Kingdom is repeated often throughout the gospel stories. They are accompanied, too, by the casting out of forces opposed to God's Kingdom plan. Sometimes these forces manifest themselves in sickness; at other times, they are seen in violent situations and in aggressive behaviour.

148. Isaiah 26:17, 35:5-6, 42:1-18, 61:1.

Following on from Jesus' declaration that the Kingdom is immanent, he goes on to say that from the days of John the Baptist until now, the Kingdom is violently assaulted and violent ones seize it.[149] There are all kinds of ways of reading this: that people are against the Kingdom and seeking to snatch it away; that evil spirits are snatching at it in a heavenly/spiritual sense; or that Kingdom-oriented people are assertively and deliberately grabbing a hold of the Kingdom as it comes close to them. However we interpret the words for violent assault, violent ones and grabbing a hold of, this comment of Jesus, referring as it does to John's own assertiveness and also the powers that are lined up against him, reveals that the Kingdom is not only a playground where the toddler plays freely by the snake's hole but, in this day and age at least, it is a warzone.

After these words, Jesus' own battle heats up. Cultivating the earth in true Sabbath by strolling through fields with his disciples who are picking grain is prioritised over the religious version of Sabbath that says lock everything down into a holy-looking version of a command and control empire. He then demonstrates the effectiveness of Shalom wholeness by telling a man with a withered hand to stretch it out before an anti-Kingdom audience. This miraculous re-creative response to the words of Jesus reminds me of the Genesis 1 repeated line, "And it was so." The man finds his hand restored and rescued, like a sheep hauled from a pit. There follows an outbreak of good news and Matthew, the writer, comments by quoting from Isaiah that Jesus is the true Servant King: one anointed by the breath of God to

---

149. Matthew 11:12.

rule and to serve, like a new kind of Adam, who proclaims justice to the wide world.[150] A demon-possessed man who was blind and mute is then brought before Jesus. For those of us used to reading the Bible, this is a normal kind of phrase, but it actually sounds like a parody of hell on earth! Who do you know down your road or at your golf club who is demon-possessed and blind and mute? The Bible simply says, "He healed him, so that the mute man spoke and saw."[151] Suddenly Jesus' words, that this generous Kingdom is surrounded by violence and requires an assertiveness to lay a hold of it, come to life as his audience declares he is working for the Ruler of Demons. Jesus replies that his kicking out of demons is the reality that the Kingdom of God has fully arrived.

The rule of God – its subduing and its reigning – is not only counter to the corruption we experience around us, but the solution. How do we see the earth restored, people healed, relationships reconciled?

The rule of God, first given to Adam and Eve – when exercised in the spirit and character of Jesus, the new human – fully arrives, remains, reaches and reigns over whatever piece of territory comes under its authority.

---

150. Matthew 12:1-21.
151. Matthew 12:22-29.

Selah, pause, reflect

What does a real hero look like?

Daniel used apocalyptic language to describe it; Jesus told stories. How might you explain the spiritual battle that you are in, that surrounds people and places and even nations?

What would you like Perez to look like in your life?

Hope deferred

This kind of rule is not the benign waving of a magic sceptre. Jesus, like John the Baptist, is assertive and courageous. Cultivating the garden in a warzone takes guts and ingenuity, and protecting it means to lay down one's life for your friend. Jesus continues to talk about this casting-out, Kingdom-arriving battle by saying that if there is a strongman guarding the house, then first this strongman needs to be bound before the house and its contents redeemed.

This is why there is such confusion and despair over our hope for the Kingdom. Like John the Baptist, we see its goodness all around and yet we continue to experience its opposite. We know deep down the human desire for the flourishing of Shalom and yet we are caught up in the thorns and thistles that simply will not be subdued. The Kingdom brings release to many, and yet even Jesus' close friends are violently assaulted one by one.

That is also why we give up so easily on the Kingdom coming to earth. It is easier to think that it exists in another place, untouched by human hands and one day accessible to those with white robes. It is much harder to believe that this Kingdom can come to the earth and make a difference, when so often its seeds of life are snatched away, or exhausted in the heat, or choked to death by every other easier, less contentious life possibility. So we soon grow tired of hoping, and although our vision for a new paradise city does not entirely leave us, it becomes a dream or an ideal. T S Eliot's *Ash Wednesday* begins in this way:

Because I do not hope to turn again
Because I do not hope
Because I do not hope to turn
Desiring this man's gift and that man's scope
I no longer strive to strive towards such things
(Why should the aged eagle stretch its wings?)
Why should I mourn
The vanished power of the usual reign?[152]

These fluctuations between hope and despair are best subdued and brought into line as we grasp more fully what Jesus means when he says that the "time is fulfilled", or that "the Kingdom of God has come upon you", or "your Kingdom come".[153] As the Kingdom of Heaven has always been God's plan for the earth, then at some point we should expect to see it and experience it. If it is a plan of God – however open, generous and in partnership with free-willed people – then it will be fulfilled. Obviously the disaster in the garden derailed this plan, but it did not stop glimpses of the Kingdom in human behaviour and in the actions of God from being expressed and stretched towards. It becomes a strategy and a vision in the Old Testament, a blueprint requiring the first foundation stone to be laid in order for it to become a reality. When Jesus came, he announced that after all this waiting and longing and preparation, the time was now fulfilled; the Kingdom had arrived. And yet, even after this announcement, each time he worked according to heavenly culture he said the Kingdom was there and then coming upon the earth, attaining its purpose. So it was still in the process of arriving. And in the prayer he taught his disciples, he told them to pray for the Kingdom to yet

---

152. Eliot, T. S. *Collected Poems, 1909-1962*. London: Faber & Faber, 1963.
153. Mark 1:15, Matthew 12:28, Matthew 6:10.

come. That is to be shown, to be established and public, in their lives and into the future.

These three kinds of 'comings' have been debated by scholars. Some scholars have identified Jesus' first proclamation as one that was an announcement that the Kingdom was just arriving, nearly here but not quite yet. One term given to this is consistent or thoroughgoing eschatology; the new Kingdom coming at the end of time was introduced by Jesus but not yet experienced.[154] A different interpretation is a realised eschatology where the coming is interpreted very much as 'has come', so that the Kingdom had already begun in its new form in the ministry of Jesus. Another variation is called a self-realising eschatology, where the plan of God's Kingdom has been gradually unfolding through history and through Jesus' announcement, and will go on being established into the future. Another helpful view is that when Jesus announced the Kingdom, it was a decisive turning point in the battle for the rule of the earth. Just as D-Day was a turning point in World War II, so was Jesus' life, death and resurrection the turning point for the Kingdom of Heaven in world history. And, as WWII was finally ended on V-E Day, so we anticipate this declaration of victory in the future, while still living now in the consequence of the decisive heavenly triumph. This explains the variety of 'times' of victory and announcements of peace and how these are experienced in reality on earth.[155]

Suffice to say, a new Kingdom arrived with the Servant King, the one who lived as Adam should. It continued to be

---

154. For all these theories, see F. F Bruce's helpful overview, "Eschatology," London
    Quarterly & Holborn Review 183 (April 1958): 99-103.
155. Cullmann, Oscar. *Christ and Time*. Oregon: Wipf and Stock, 2018.

expressed through his words and deeds and acts of power. And the New Testament writers tell of how there will be a completion and a filling up of the heavenly rule of God on the earth, as God lives with mankind, and mankind reigns well through Jesus. These beginnings, continuings and expectations reveal how we live in a tension of experiencing the Kingdom of Heaven as a new recreation in all kinds of lovely and even unusual ways, while also experiencing the attacking of and grasping at this same Godly rule.

Its not easy to live in the 'now and not yet'. In the same way as I prepare for my Greek island holiday, having bought my ticket and now buying suntan cream, eating olives and baklava and practicing snorkeling at my local leisure centre, I live truly in hope that I will actually be there soon. This is quite different to the vain wish that I were somewhere sunny and hot, without having any evidence that I am already halfway there. Living in hope is not wishful. It is the confidence in and present experience of that which is anticipated.

The encouragement given to us in the New Testament is 'don't give up'. The pressure of experiencing one culture and yearning for another often gives rise either to an angst or a lowering of expectations and even a giving up on the vision. Remaining in a tense state of expectation means that hope twists out of shape and may just become a psychological protection from the realities of pain. If we are not careful, we may ignore all that is already good around us and write off everything as disappointingly less than our own judgement of what should be. Such tension also tends to lead us towards an otherworldly wishfulness that takes up time and energy better spent on cultivating and keeping what is already here.

Alternatively, we may give up on the Kingdom and bow the knee to the immediate and self-centred benefits of empire life. St. Paul writes about this to the church at Corinth, reminding them that Israel, the family of families, drank the refreshing water of the river of God. In the tension of freedom having happened but still yet to fully happen, they craved a more immediate fix. He describes those of us who wait as those "upon whom the ends of the ages have come".[156] This explains the pressure of a new age of the Kingdom of Heaven reigning fully on earth and in heaven, while an existing dominion of sickness, injustice and disappointment also exercises its power. We are caught in between these two rules. But, like yeast through dough, the Kingdom of Heaven is already glimpsed in every person and creature and day. It is seen arriving in its recreating newness in Jesus and continuing to arrive every time its culture of justice, peace and joy pushes out death, selfishness and misery. And it will one day fully arrive in the form of "a new heaven and a new earth", the garden city packed full of mankind's and God's treasured possessions. [157]

Selah, pause, reflect

Acts of love can cause violent reactions. This is the corrupted cosmos in which we live. Many of the psalms are about experiencing this tension. How have you experienced the 'now and not yet' of the Kingdom of Heaven? What does it make you feel?

---

156. 1 Corinthians 10:1-11
157. Revelation 21:1.

The parables of Jesus – Seeds and Flourishings in the Kingdom

We have seen how different the culture of the Kingdom is to that which we are used to. This is especially true in its approach to justice through sacrificial love and its trust in the power of love, however small and insignificantly this is expressed.

Jesus' parables of the Kingdom are often about what is small and insignificant becoming increasingly and unmanageably (in a fun way) large. These stories show us a great deal about the culture of the Kingdom, not least in the fact that they are unusual, quirky and puzzling stories rather than government white papers or chalkboards of equations. The Kingdom of Heaven is characterised by tragedy, comedy and fairy tale.[158] Not that Jesus' parables are just the stuff of West End musicals, but they reveal that the Kingdom has the attributes of theatre and story. In the way that tragedy, comedy and fairytale make us yearn for growth, completion, beauty and justice, the parables reflect the big story and the many stories of the Kingdom of Heaven.

Seeds

Genesis is about seeds and beginnings. This is the small beginnings of animals, people and a garden, and the promise of a new family that will fill the earth. It is the

---

158. Buechner, Frederick. *Telling the Truth: The Gospel of Comedy, Tragedy and Fairytale.* New York: Harper, 1977.

woman's seed that will produce the one seed who will overcome the serpent's curse. It is Abraham's seed that will begin as Sarah's cackling laughter but eventually becomes as majestically song-filled as the stars in the universe.

The most significant story of Jesus about the Kingdom is the Parable of the Sower.[159] This is found in Matthew, Mark and Luke's gospels and is given a meaning by Jesus, a key to understand not just this parable but any parable.

The story has within it many Kingdom characteristics. A seed, even in its tiny size, contains within it all the attributes of its mother plant and the potential not just to grow itself into maturity but to multiply according to its kind. A seed is therefore small but also very large indeed in its scope and possibility. The Kingdom of Heaven, even when it is small, has productive power to spread and lead to abundance. The sower is active and generous. The King of the Kingdom is not impassive or in a waiting limbo, but treading creation and scattering hope and life. There is opposition to the Kingdom of Heaven: whether this is because of a resistant context that is stamped down hard over years of ignorance, or subject to an external grabbing by violent ones, or at the mercy of old comfortable patterns of slavery which appear more satisfying and accessible than the riskily attempted grace-notes of the Kingdom of Heaven. The end of the story promises a superabundance; an overflow that seems to bear no realistic relation to the small amount of investment initially made. If the seed of Kingdom love is planted or experienced well, then the immense fruitfulness that is within it has no bounds.

---

159. Matthew 13:1-23, Mark 4:1-20, Luke 8:1-15.

Like a mustard seed planted in a field

This story is told by Matthew, Mark and Luke with some slight and interesting variations.[160] Mustard seed is a domestic image. The Kingdom of Heaven is not compared to palaces and chauffeur driven cars. It is experienced in everyday life. Luke describes a man throwing this seed in his garden, which is casual homely scene. Mustard seed was used as a medicine (even until recently in England) to draw out fever as a poultice. The English word mustard means 'hot wine' and it is also used in some cultures to ward off evil spirits.[161] As part of the cabbage and rapeseed family, as a biofuel, it has a huge calorific content. Pliny wrote in AD 78 that "mustard . . . is extremely beneficial for the health. It grows entirely wild, though it is improved by being transplanted: but on the other hand when it has once been sown it is scarcely possible to get the place free of it, as the seed when it falls germinates at once".[162] A mustard seed is not necessarily the smallest seed, and as a plant it is not necessarily the largest tree, but it does have weed-like properties and grows hugely to over 2 metres tall in a messy, unkempt and voracious way. Jesus' use of hyperbole gives strength to this image. The Kingdom of Heaven is at home being 'at home'. It is tiny but packed full of medicinal, flavoursome, spiritual power and energetic qualities.

We have seen the importance of the image of the tree in the Bible – from the garden to the city. It is used as an image of the strength of earthly Kingdoms. Israel, Assyria,

---

160. Matthew 13:31-32; Mark 4:30-32; Luke 13:18-19.
161. Mustard is made up of two Latin words: mustum (grape must) and ardens (burning). See *The Cambridge World History of Food* by Kenneth F Kiple and Kriemhild Conee Omelas, Cambridge UP, 2000.
162. Cited by Cameron Freeman in *Post-metaphysics and the Paradoxical Teachings of Jesus: The Structure of the Real*. Bern: Peter Lang, 2010.

Egypt and Babylon are all majestically treelike, but in their pride may well get chopped down.[163] Trees are like mountains in that they are firmly rooted on the earth, and yet tower towards the heavens. They are as heavenly as they are earthly and provide a home for both creatures and birds. The Kingdom of God similarly joins heaven and earth together. Jesus alludes to one of these tree pictures found at the end of Ezekiel 17 and also in the writing of Daniel, where Nebudchanezzar's reign is like a tree where the birds of the air come and nest in his branches.[164] Although some say that Jesus is referring to evil elements that find themselves encircling the kingdom, the fact that this allusion is from Daniel is a very positive affirmation of a good kingdom. That these birds are nesting and therefore at home and even reproducing seems to indicate that one of the roles of the Kingdom tree is to provide a safe habitat for all people, and for spiritual beings whose habitat is the heavens.

Seeds and weeds, roots and shoots

The remarkable growth of a seed becoming a reproducing plant is a helpful comparison to the mystery of the Kingdom's growth. The Kingdom is like a man who sows seed and then goes to bed, and it is during this Sabbath rest, when we are helpless and inactive, that the Kingdom continues to grow. There is a time when we can't see its evidence, in fact our experience is at times bleak and disappointing, but the promise of God's rule is that where it is planted it will grow, even without us necessarily cultivating it.[165]

---

163. Ezekiel 17, Ezekiel 31.
164. Daniel 4:10-17. Ezekiel 17:23 is also a positive prophetic picture of the Shalom habitat of God's tree.
165. Mark 4:26-29.

It is not only the lack of evidence that can be frustrating, but the Kingdom grows in the midst of a different culture that is also doing its own growing. In this way, it is like a field where weeds are growing among the wheat crop. In our tendency towards exercising our own judgements, Jesus compares us to workers who want to pull up the weeds as soon as possible. But the Kingdom is meant to grow on the earth surrounded by all kinds of other plants. Overzealous religion actually uproots and destroys the life it is wanting to preserve. The Kingdom of Heaven is not meant to be put aside in a greenhouse or a special sacred shrine. It is designed to grow on earth and across the heavens, and its harvesting is a God thing rather than a human thing.[166]

Hidden and secret

The parables of the mustard seed, and the farmer who goes to bed after sowing, both hint at the hidden secret workings of the Kingdom of Heaven. Typically, a kingdom will show itself with plenty of pomp, PR and advertising. It promotes itself and its image is often greater than its reality. The Kingdom of Heaven is different in that it points towards others, or its pointing is about its own simplicity. It points towards the King who "has no stately form or majesty that we should look upon Him, nor appearance that we should be attracted to Him".[167] It does not need PR and flashing lights to show what it has done. Its doing is its strength and integrity. This is the simplicity of design. It is the mustard tree that ends up being a haven for the birds of the air, rather than the splendid cypress tree entered for Best in Show. The seeds under the ground are invisibly working,

---

166. Matthew 13:24-30.
167. Isaiah 53:2.

not intending to just grow into large plants that look good, but instead to sprout: first the blade, then the head, then the grain in the head, which is food for the farmer.

Another hidden working parable is the Parable of the Leaven. In a similar way to the mustard seed story, this is a domestic picture. The Kingdom is like a woman, not a powerful male King, who makes bread rather than driving a Ferrari or being a successful hedge fund manager. She is handling yeast, which in Jesus' culture was unclean and not very godly, rather than handling theological hardbacks or government white papers. There is a lot of dough but not much yeast, and yet the yeast makes the whole dough rise. Initially it looks insignificant, if not messy and even despicable. It works its way. It is effective. It transforms.[168]

What makes a good harvest?

This harvest is clearly something that most of us want to be in on: planning, determining, weighing. There is a natural human tendency to want to decide what's best – for others, for the earth, for God. But the Kingdom of Shalom in its fullness is expressed with relationships of peace and satisfaction, rather than by a telephone vote for who stays for the final and who gets thrown out. This doesn't mean that there is no judgement in the Kingdom. It is all about judging and measuring and declaring what works well and what doesn't. Nevertheless, where religion has a tendency towards trying to make everything as holy as possible – presumably so that when our life project is examined, we won't lose too many marks – the Kingdom has a tendency

168. Matthew 13:33.

to embrace every weed, slug, octopus and shopping trolley as its dragnet sweeps along the murky rubbish-strewn floor, catching everything in its grace embrace. And just like in that first week of creation, it is God who will say what is good, what is not good and what is very good.[169]

Whereas Jesus shows in these Kingdom parables this judging is God's job and we should get on with cultivating and protecting, he does have some instructions for how we should be ready for a judgement. At the end of Matthew's gospel, Jesus tells stories about our attitudes towards the King. A life of celebration and anticipation could become a doped drowsy ignorance, even while the banquet is on the table and the disco is thumping.[170] What we have been given is invested with hope and creative ingenuity, or buried in resentment and rebellion.[171] People are divided into sheep and goats (almost as impossible a task as dividing wheat from tares unless you are a goat expert) based not on their religious devotion, but in their pursuit of Shalom.[172] This final story feels as much like a prophetic reality as a parable, where the Kingdom of Heaven is the natural culture for those who already are desiring Shalom – by feeding, inviting, clothing, and visiting. None of these activities are particularly miraculous or seemingly powerful; there isn't any talk of even setting prisoners free or healing. Instead, the only thing that counts is faith expressing itself though love.

---

169. Matthew 13:47-50.
170. Matthew 25:1-13.
171. Matthew 25:14-30.
172. Matthew 25:31-46.

Parables of Jesus –
Feasts and Tables

Inviting in

True to the festivals of Shalom, Jesus compares the Kingdom of Heaven to a feast. He models this in his habit of spending time eating meals with friends and even enemies. In fact it is unusual, and therefore remarked upon by gospel writers, for him not to eat. Jesus eats with the poor and with those who made the poor, poor. He eats with those who work for the Roman Empire and with those whose lifestyles are utterly despised. He eats with religious people and with large crowds where everyone is represented.

The Kingdom strategy of the Old Testament paved the way for an understanding of the Kingdom as a banquet. We have already seen how Shalom and wellbeing is not just about the absence of disease but about the presence of celebration and feasting. The family of families was designed around a series of feasts. Worship was essentially a feast, whether that was in the sacrifices or in the special holidays that brought everyone together to eat and relax. After meeting a Roman Centurion who understands the Kingdom like no one else, Jesus says that the Kingdom is like a feast where people from all over the globe will eat with the big eaters, Abraham, Isaac and Jacob.[173]

Many of Jesus' parables are about feasts. There is the Parable of the Wedding Feast where those invited have

---

173. Matthew 8:5-13.

mundane, anxiety ridden reasons not to come.[174] The Kingdom here is like a party where the concerns of everyday life can be left with the coats and bags at the entrance to Sabbath, so that the enjoyment is not simply about what has been well earned but what has been gracefully received. It takes faith and security to receive and to be well treated, because in the usual systems of empire there is no such thing as a free lunch, and at some point payment will be required. In our karma culture, we have got used to the confident reassurance that comes with paying for our own meal: no-one can then catch us out or accuse us. In the Kingdom, however, we have to put our confidence and trust in the character of the King who will not turn round and bite us or demand payment.

The parable does not finish with everyone refusing the free meal or the chance to celebrate. Others are invited to the feast: those who really don't deserve a place there, the hangers on, the deceivers, the wasters and the freeloaders. And also the ones who no-one ever invites to such events because it is too awkward; they carry in their bodies a reminder of misery and pain, there is absolutely no way that these people can then return the invitation at a later date. All these later guests have every reason to desperately rely on the grace of the King. They have no other means of payment.

Ironically, in Matthew's version of the story, there is a man not dressed in wedding clothes. He is thrown out. This appears contrary to the command to invite people in off the streets who obviously wouldn't be dressed for the

---

174. Matthew 22:1-14, Luke 14:15-24.

occasion. Surely we are not back to rules and regulations in the Kingdom of Heaven?

God's own clothes are the light of the sky and he is covered in the man-fashioned, earth-made tabernacle.[175] God's attitude to creation and the Kingdom is one of delight and honour. Through the story of God and man, God has a habit of making clothes for people. Whether this is Adam and Eve, Aaron, Joshua the High Priest – in the Kingdom there is always a covering for us to wear that overcomes shame and reflects and restores our God-given glory. The clothing the guest is refusing to wear is more about his attitude to the feast than golf club bylaws. Paul writes: "Therefore, as God's chosen people, holy and dearly loved, clothe yourselves with compassion, kindness, humility, gentleness and patience."[176] It is back to the qualities of Shalom rather than dress to impress. The man is dumbstruck, his speechlessness is like the stilling of the storm raging against Jesus and his disciples, or the muzzling of the shouting demons who oppose Jesus. His is a conscious rebellion against peace and justice. There is no longer room for arrogant posturing in the Kingdom.

Pouring out

The Kingdom of Heaven is a free invitation to all those who have been poured out or have poured themselves out. It is free to people who are empty or have been emptied. In fact, the emptier you are, the more room there is for food. Or, as Jesus put it, the more there is to be forgiven,

---

175. Psalm 104.
176. Colossians 3:12.

the more thankful is your heart.[177] Paul, using Jesus' description of his own life, as his blood is poured out for many, describes himself as one who has been poured out, like an offering. This line comes after a poem that he writes about Jesus the Servant King who "although He existed in the form of God, did not regard equality with God a thing to be grasped, but emptied Himself, taking the form of a bondservant, and being made in the likeness of men. Being found in appearance as a man, He humbled Himself by becoming obedient to the point of death, even death on a cross. For this reason also, God highly exalted Him, and bestowed on Him the name which is above every name, so that at the name of Jesus every knee will bow, of those who are in heaven and on earth and under the earth, and that every tongue will confess that Jesus Christ is Lord, to the glory of God the Father."[178]

This emptying is at the heart of the culture of the Kingdom, ironically a culture that is all about filling up and multiplying! It appears that the route to fullness is via humble pouring out. Perhaps this is what we saw when God, stooping low, breathed into Adam the breath of life. Such self-giving is certainly spoken of later when God declares he will pour out his spirit onto everyone on the earth. Jesus came to serve because it is serving and protecting that causes the garden to flourish. He poured out his blood for many because he knew that to gain life it is necessary to lose one's life. "Truly, truly, I say to you, unless a grain of wheat falls into the earth and dies, it remains alone; but if it dies, it bears much fruit."[179] In all four gospels, Jesus is recorded to have

---

177. Luke 7:41-43.
178. Philippians 2:6-11.
179. John 12:24.

said, "For whoever wants to save their life will lose it, but whoever loses their life for me will save it."[180] The wine of the feast of the Kingdom of Heaven is not for pride of place, laser protected pedestal display, sitting "on its dregs" as Jeremiah puts it, but for pouring out, breaking forth, giving away drinking.[181]

A seat at the table

Jesus also compares the Kingdom to treasure that is hidden in a field. Someone stumbles on it accidentally but then realises its worth and gives up everything for it. Their response is a self-giving in the light of the enormous worth of the Kingdom of Heaven. Similarly, it is like a beautiful pearl. This time the finder has been actively seeking this kind of pearl and when they find it, they too give everything up. Whether the Kingdom has been a quest that up till now has not been fully realised, or whether its discovery is a chance affair, the response to its quality is the same.[182] The Kingdom of Heaven is the seed of life. Who wouldn't seek the Kingdom first, if the Kingdom of Heaven is actually all that we have deep down longed for?

Wealth and power are wonderful to have, as they are our usual access to the life we have always wanted. It is a life of Shalom, perhaps somewhat tainted by a need to exert ourselves or compensate at last for things that have not gone so well. But generally wealth and power (and our sexuality as influence and connection) enable us to find seats at most tables. In the Kingdom of Heaven, if self-emptying, humility and sacrifice are what characterise

---

180. Matthew 16:25; Mark 8:35; Luke 9:24; John 12:25.
181. Jeremiah 48:11.
182. Matthew 13:44-46.

God's household economics, then wealth and power may not be the right currency. A child, who is without wealth and power, and whose sexuality is as likely to be abused as protected, is a great image of one who will inherit the Kingdom, especially as God sees His Kingdom more as a family and a household than a palace. God is a Father, not an emperor, which probably explains why love is pre-eminent in His Kingdom rather than might. A child belongs to the family simply because they were born into it. They have brought nothing with them apart from a hungry stomach and a loud voice.

It is no surprise, then, that Jesus says we must be like children to enter the Kingdom of Heaven.[183] Of course children can be as annoying, competitive and defensive as adults, but before these things have solidified in their souls there is an innocence and a hope that reflects God's reign. It makes sense that Jesus says to Nicodemus that one must be born again to see and enter the Kingdom of God.[184] He wasn't necessarily meaning the saying of a particular prayer at this point. Rather, if the Kingdom is a family and God is the Father, then to be in the family you need to be a child, to be adopted in and to take the Father's DNA so that you really are like His Son, Jesus. This cannot be bought, or earned with power or even hard work.

A rich young ruler – one who had wealth, power and had not quite yet aged crooked – asked Jesus how he might enter the Kingdom.[185] (He knew that the quality of life promised in the Kingdom was to be desired, so he phrased

---

183. Matthew 18:3.
184. John 3:3.
185. Luke 18:18-27.

this as 'having eternal life'.) Jesus' challenge to him was to give up self-oriented control and come in not as one who had achieved full marks in the 10 commandments pub quiz, or was deserving because of his religious living, but as one who was empty but hungry. Riches make it particularly hard for someone to find the Kingdom, not because of a lack of integrity, or obedience, or diligence, but because they can undermine childlike trust and dependency. Riches of all kinds will be brought into the Kingdom, and they do often accompany those who have excelled in subduing and ruling. And because these attributes are good, riches are not ignored for being too complex in their origin, or tainted beyond cleansing. The answer, as with everything in the Kingdom, is to give them. It is more blessed that way.

So, if we come like a child, empty-handed, will we be given those top seats? Who is the greatest in the Kingdom?

This is probably a meaningless question. Jesus is greatest because he became the least. But he didn't become the least so he could then be the greatest. He became the least because he loved to serve others. So then being made the greatest is fine, but actually doesn't change his desire to carry on serving and loving and walking the earth through his body, the church.

He is always the child, the Son of God, dependent on his father. He is always the self-emptying one who cultivates and protects. The top seats at the wedding table are given by God to whomever he pleases. They may remain unoccupied at times because whoever has them keeps leaving them to wash people's feet or fill up the wine, or dry the dishes or direct traffic in the car park. Perhaps there will be too much going on to bother about these positions, and we will have so many invitations to sit under our neighbour's fig tree that we will need to stretch our legs and work off the cake and puddings, rather than sit splendidly on thrones. And given that these seats are thrones, they are not actually places for those who have lobbied for reward or consideration, rather they are places of responsibility. At his last feast with his disciples, Jesus was happy to say to his friends that his ambition was for them to eat and drink at his table in His Kingdom.[186] Therefore, we probably will want to sit there, but only because we love to play within the order and the surprise of God's universe. The heavens and the earth will always need good governance, whether it is to umpire Gabriel's first XI versus a bunch of posh Victorian social reformers, or to calibrate the settings in our hot tub. And being seated with the King in heavenly places is also a great place from which to live and move here on the earth, because this is where he rests his feet.

Selah, pause, reflect

Have you ever thought why did Jesus explain the Kingdom through parables rather than a definitive textbook?

Think through the stories of Jesus that are annoying, obtuse, confusing or have bits in that feel wrong and unjust.

What stories, tales and fables in your culture have strong elements of the Kingdom of Heaven in them?

---

186. Luke 22:28-30.

The Kingdom of Death and Resurrection

The word gospel is a political, new-world term. It is proclaimed to groups of people and not just shared with individuals. It is the news that there is a victory and that now is the time to celebrate with a party. The gospel comes with immediate power and with a gradual transforming influence. It is contested and a place of battle. It has arrived in all its newness in Jesus but is still coming and will one day arrive fully. The gospel of the Kingdom has as its culture sacrifice and self-giving generosity. It begins with vulnerable seeds that contain within them life that can multiply. It is often hidden and secret but eventually brings transformation and shelter to the whole earth. In the story of God it is good news for the earth and heavens.

Where does this leave our traditional understanding that the gospel is primarily about an individual's destiny, the new spiritual life given to them through the death and resurrection of Jesus? So much of Jesus' time was in intimate conversation with men and women as they wrestled with the challenge of living in a new realm. John's gospel has a number of stories of individual lifechanging encounters with Jesus, and in conversation with Nicodemus as he talks about the Kingdom, the classic phrase "born again" is used.[187] And so much of the writing of Paul also describe the incredible effect that the King has on those who find themselves in the Kingdom. Paul is described as preaching the Kingdom of God at the end of the Book of Acts – he is

---

187. John 3:3.

no less subversive in his approach to the empire of Rome or the tradition of the Jews, both worlds he fully inhabits – but in his letters he uses some different terminology to that of Jesus. He uses the term Christ, itself a Greek form of Messiah or anointed one, sent by God to rule the earth. He is well known for the way he describes what it means to be a new creation in Christ, destined for heavenly living.

But this gospel is no more individualistic or otherworldly than the gospel of Genesis 1, of the family that blesses families, of Shalom, or of the Kingdom of Heaven.

When Paul describes Jesus ascending as King, leading the captives with him and giving gifts to men,[188] he is quoting from an excitable psalm of praise where God is living on the earth as a father to the fatherless and a judge for the widows, a host for the lonely and a leader of prisoners reigning over a land where the poor are provided for.[189] Paul goes on to say, "Now this expression, 'He ascended,' what does it mean except that He also had descended into the lower parts of the earth? He who descended is Himself also He who ascended far above all the heavens, so that He might fill all things."[190]

This journey of Jesus, from the highest place to the lowest place, is at the heart of the Good News of the Kingdom. It demonstrates that where the earth was corrupted and the Kingdom plan derailed, that God had it in Him to put it back on track without changing his loving nature. The fact that Jesus came to serve and get his hands dirty, breathe new life into old bones, rule over and subdue the earth, restore

---

188. Ephesians 4:7-13.
189. Psalm 68.
190. Ephesians 4:9-10.

back hearts and relationships to one another and to God, and then give up power and even end up murdered – this reflects all the values of the culture of the Kingdom. His story is not alien to the big Kingdom plan but fleshes it out perfectly in the life of a human being. What Paul refers to is that Jesus ascending must mean that at some point he is pretty low down. He is at the bottom of the table. He is kicked outside of the feast and even the city. The death of Jesus is not necessarily just an anti-Kingdom victory for the anti-Christ, but it was also a chosen path, because a seed has to die before it sprouts into life. The corruption that was holding people and even the earth and heavens in its grip needed destroying.

Therefore the death of Jesus is as significant as the life he lived, the works he did and the words he said. It is his ultimate act of sacrificial love and debt freeing Jubilee. It is Jesus emptying himself of every part of life – heavenly and earthly – so that he has truly given everything, and so that he truly has to depend on the fact that God is either full of grace and goodness . . . or not. That the King of the Kingdom should die is awful, but strangely makes sense in an upside down kingdom where the greatest are the least and the last are the first. If even the King can lose his life then he is not as power-grabbing and insecure as every other king I've ever known after all. And then to see that God the Creator Father brings back to life this blooded, sin-covered, humiliated brokenness means that the same can happen to people, animals, the earth, seas and heavens. That Jesus forgives is a weird thing for a King to do. Kings have to protect themselves by not forgiving but slaughtering. The Kingdom of Heaven has a different nature, so when Jesus then rises from the dead, with a forgiving heart and the power of something death defying in his breath, then whatever happened in the garden that brought death is reversed, or broken, or defused. It is the moment when the wheels of crushing fate that have been oppressing everything in their path have finally slowed to a stop and they begin to turn the other way. A new fate or magic begins to work, the polarity is reversed, and a new ethos river flows. In Genesis, God said that the serpent would bite Jesus' heel, but that Jesus (the new seed) would crush the serpent's head. This is what happened when Jesus died: a crushing of anti-Kingdom power, but through love and humility rather than a bigger stick, tank or warship.

Oddly, this power was crushed through Jesus himself being crushed, and somehow the responsibility of the whole of humanity was transferred to his willing but wounded new-Adam shoulders. Just as Adam and Eve were covered by God in their first shame, and the earth covered by a cleansing flood, and the ark covered by a protecting water resistant tar, and sacrifices covered in a substitute's blood, so Jesus was covered in his own blood and brought a covering for everyone's failure of responsibility to subdue and rule well, or tendency to domineer and exploit instead of protect and serve. The covering clothes that he gives us now are the wedding clothes of those who are part of the new Kingdom culture.

The death of Jesus is a closing of a door on what has been and destroying what is behind that door. The rising of Jesus is the opening of a new door, where all kinds of things are possible that surely were not before. Changes of heart and behaviour, healing of sicknesses, ability to work together to serve, compassion and action on behalf of the earth, even walking on water and most of all, the possibility that the heavens will come to the earth after all and that the knowledge of the glory of the Lord will cover the earth. This all happens as Jesus rises and ascends. Interestingly, in quoting that psalm, Paul changes the words. Where, usually the king would ascend and receive gifts from men, which would be expected in any self-respecting empire whether Jewish, Roman or Western, in this Kingdom the King gives out gifts to people as he ascends. Primarily this is the gift of new life; the same life that reversed the curse in Jesus is now available to reverse the curse in the rest of the cosmos. These are also the gifts that will strengthen and grow into maturity the body of Christ, the new humanity.

Where Paul often uses the term Christ to mean the anointed King and the reign of the Kingdom, John uses a special word for life, Zoe. Not simply biological life, but a quality of life or the spark of life that is in humanity and animals. John says Jesus described his mission as bringing a super abundance of this kind of life. It is Living the Life, it is This is the Life, it is Choose Life. The life of the Kingdom is not a life of religious obsequiousness (scrabble style word meaning servile compliance), but it is about life to the full.

After rising up from the depths of the earth, Jesus is recorded as giving this kind of life away to his friends by breathing on them and saying receive my Spirit.[191] The spirit is also life – we can't live without breath – and the Holy Spirit is the breath of God, breathing those life words at creation, and of course being breathed into Adam so that he stands up and becomes a living being. In fact, these

---

191. John 20:22.

two breathings into humans are like two Creation Kingdom moments. The first kicks off life and sets up Adam for his cultivating and protecting. The second is a new version of this. This same life is breathed by Jesus into broken people, giving them the same authority to rule well and see the fullness of Kingdom life once again fill up the earth and the heavens.

Both of these breathings sandwich a third event where God breathes into people, which is a vision in the book of Ezekiel. Here, in a valley of bones where all life has gone, word and breath life is spoken into the skeletons and they stand up, fit together and receive life once more.[192] This is strikingly similar to the Word and the Breath of God bringing life into the cosmos in Genesis 1. The vision continues with an explicit description of the Kingdom of Heaven on the earth. Just as with Adam and with Jesus' friends, God says that he will put his spirit in people and they will come to life and live in their own land. They will have a King, like King David. They will have a covenant of Shalom and God will live among them on the earth. It sounds like a vision of the Kingdom that is coming. At this point, when Ezekiel prophesies, it is a hope and a promise, but when Jesus comes as a new King David, with the breath of God in his mouth that hovers over chaotic waters, and the word of God on his lips that speaks life into existence, then it looks at last like the Kingdom has come.

---

192. Ezekiel 37:1-28.

Selah, pause, reflect

Therefore, the gospel of the Kingdom is of course the good news that Jesus died and then rose again from the dead, and so reclaimed Zoe life for himself, humanity and the whole of creation. This may make some sense to individuals as they see how it applies to the life of their own souls and their place in the everlasting Kingdom of God, but that is certainly not all. Some listeners may well say "So what?"

After declaring that Jesus died and rose from the dead, we must go on to say, "So that . . ."

So that individuals would be in relationship with God at the wedding feast wearing new-culture clothes.
So that many more bodies would be healed and broken hearts restored.
So that the poor would continue to have the good news preached to them in every place and at every time.
So that those in debt, bondage and captivity would go free.
So that the dark forces of evil that grip people in depression, or sweep up whole groups into violently oppressing others, would be kicked out and disarmed.
So that justice and peace would be proclaimed, lived out and spread in families, communities and nations.
So that the earth and its creatures would not be exploited and abused, but well looked after and cultivated.
So that the new city would come out of heaven and join all that has been built well on the earth.

So that God himself would finally come, not for an evening, or for an occasional meal, or in once place at one time, but everywhere in every place among every person, and the heavens and the earth would join together in a loving union and a feast of food, life and activity.

Part 4

Prophets, Priests and Kings

When we talk of a Kingdom we will of course be talking about governance and the nurturing of a culture. This is evident in the ruling language of Genesis 1 and the shepherding language of Genesis 2. Jesus the Servant King picks up these vocabularies and we see them in many other parts of the Bible. We can easily see how our everyday lives, however challenged, have within them the capacity and opportunity to shepherd and rule, to bring an order and a peace to the material and relational worlds in which we dwell.

Nevertheless, the Bible is less often seen as the story of the Kingdom of Heaven, and more often interpreted as the development of a religion and a route towards a post-death spiritual heavenly existence. The stories of priests, prophets and kings in the Bible are often retold to describe this religious way of life and point the way to another, better more ethereal world.

The role of the priest is to connect with the God of heaven and mediate between this God and mankind and the earth. The priest's activities include sacrifices and rituals, most often in a special place or temple. Priests in the Bible are sometimes very fat, sometimes petty and sometimes respected. The role of the prophet is to know the wisdom of God, hear the voice of God and then deliver this to God's people and especially his rulers, and also to other nations and rulers around. The prophets in the Bible are often feared by kings and people, behave and dress oddly and may tend towards misery. The role of the king is to rule on behalf of God as a good example of a human being who brings justice, care and prosperity to their kingdom. The kings in the Bible are often violent warlords or scaredy-cats who seem more interested in pretty women than good governance. Their increasingly poor rule contrasts with the permanence of the priesthood and the emergence of powerfully vocal prophetic voices. Perhaps it is the failure of the kings, overshadowing even the diligent rule of God-appointed civil servants, which deflects our view away from the Kingdom being about managing well life on earth, towards religion and its escape to a more perfect spiritual existence.

Although Genesis 1 and 2 are about the fullness of life, by the time Jesus talks about abundant life we are more likely to interpret this as 'spiritual' instead of an actual here and now existence. But the story of God and His people – the family of families who gather around him and invite other peoples into the new nation – is not meant to be split into these two opposing perspectives. In fact, the priesthood and the temple are pictures and examples of what the Kingdom of Heaven should look and feel like. They are meant to be pictures of an everyday life of reconciliation and heaven-and earth-connectivity. The prophets are a continuation of that creative voice of God, bringing vision that can become reality on earth. They encourage the kings by assertively laying hold of heaven and making its truth and power available in everyday life and in the corridors of political power. Their vision of the future, along with the temple pattern woven into the fabric of earthly life, reveals the long-range plan of the Kingdom of Heaven on the earth.

Jesus as Prophet,
Priest and King

Jesus' life and ministry does not ignore the priestly and prophetic in favour of His Kingdom-living manifesto. He is certainly not a mad hairy figure living on the edge of society, and neither is he a stern and demanding cleric. His familiarity means that he is approachable and his indictment of the religious leaders and rulers sets him at odds with the temple system of his day. But he himself fulfils the roles of prophet and priest as well as being the king of a new Kingdom. And what this means is that these roles point towards the significance of, and are themselves a part of, life in the Kingdom of Heaven even now.

Jesus is a prophet. He stands up to people in power. He speaks truth into the lives of individuals and he declares God's intentions for his generation and for humanity. His actions point to the Creator God whose compassions never fail. His coming as a prophet was prophesied by Moses (that great forerunner prophet, king and priest of the family of families) when he said, "The Lord your God will raise up for you a prophet like me from among you, from your countrymen, you shall listen to him."[193] After Jesus ascended, his friend Peter quotes this in his first sermon, declaring that Jesus is its fulfilment. Jesus himself says he is a prophet when he recognises that a prophet is without honour in his own town and also when he shows

---

193. Deuteronomy 18:15.

he is determined to get to Jerusalem, which is the place a prophet must die.[194] The first public appearance of Jesus, recorded in all four gospels, is when he is met by John the Baptist. John is the greatest of all prophets, the hinge between the old order and the new, but he says that Jesus is the greater one coming after him. Jesus is in the line of John the Baptist, the final fulfilment of all the prophesied words of God, summed up in what John (the gospel writer) calls the Word of God.

Jesus is also a priest. He does not work officially in the temple, not does he slaughter animals while wearing a large hat, but he fulfils the role without doing these things. If a priest is meant to mediate between God and man, then of course Jesus is doing this all the time. But his priestly acts are made more obvious because they are public. He heals, cleanses and even forgives people. This is what should happen in a temple through sacrifices. It is as if Jesus has an invisible portable temple that is erected wherever he goes. Before healing a paralysed man, he declares that his sins are forgiven, which is objected to by observers, as only God can do that, and only ordained priests could bring someone to that place of receiving such forgiveness.[195] Jesus fulfils a priestly role while at the same time breaking lots of priestly rules, which makes it difficult to assess whether he is a good priest or renegade priest. He heals a blind man but does this as 'work' on a Sabbath, making clay for the man's eyes which is also work and then asking the man to walk further than he should on a Sabbath to the pool of Siloam.[196] Jesus is a priest in the line of Melchizedek, who

---

194. Mark 6:4, Luke 13:33.
195. Mark 2:1-12.
196. John 9.

was a mysterious priest/king who brought refreshment to Abram in the form of bread and wine.[197] This of course is echoed in Jesus giving bread and wine to his friends as a covenant between God and man. Even Jesus' well-known miracle, again recorded in all four gospels, the feeding of the five thousand, is a priestly act as Jesus lifts the food towards heaven and distributes it to the people. It does not have the solemnity or gravitas of temple activities; instead, it is a celebration of outdoor picnic fun. And Jesus' own act of sacrifice is a fulfilment of all the main temple sacrifices outlined in Leviticus.

As Jesus ushers in the Kingdom of Heaven, he fulfils the role of priest and prophet. Therefore, these roles are not meant to remain in the realm of the religious but are more likely to be ways of us understanding what the Kingdom of Heaven is all about. Perhaps we have divided our earthly responsibilities and callings from what has been seen as sacred, and from a particular calling to warn, declare and convict a world which is not that much in touch with its creator king. These divisions leave people stretched and somewhat confused. If the message of the Kingdom is really all about getting people off the earth to a heavenly realm, then maybe our main objective is priestly, or to prophetically warn. We see that some are more naturally priestly than others so it becomes a particular vocation for those set apart and more devout. The prophets are edgy, political and provocative, so maybe that too is for a certain type or passionate individual. At worst, the temple and the prophets look like the most boring or most off-putting aspects of the Bible's exhortation to find God: it is just

197. Hebrews 7:1-17.

another religion after all! But what if the pictures we have in the Bible of the temple and its priests are another way of explaining God's plan for humanity to fill the earth? What if the prophets' relationship to the kings and the people is actually normative, and an essential part of the strategy to subdue the earth and rule effectively, wisely and towards Shalom? The final picture we have of the King and the Kingdom living fully on earth and in heaven at the end of the book of Revelation has no temple and no prophets but does have plenty of good ruling. In the meantime, however, the temple and the prophets are actually a blueprint and a guide – online help – for us to fulfil that ultimate vision.

Selah, pause, reflect

How does Jesus live out the roles of prophet, priest and king, even though he is a carpenter's son and hasn't trained professionally for any of those roles?

And how can you do the same?

Temple

It is important to remember that when we talk of the Kingdom of God we don't simply mean place or territory, but we mean the ruling power of God, or right of God to rule. Perhaps we should sometimes say the 'Kingship of Heaven', especially as we see certain territories that are reigned over by another ruler into which God stretches his own rule. Nevertheless, whether we talk of the place where God is and rules from, or the territory of the earth into which God's heavenly Kingdom is coming, there is a seat that is ruled from and there is a province that is ruled over. When the Kingdom is at war, there would seem to be a tension between these two 'places' but when the Kingdom is at peace, the seat and the domain are seamlessly connected.

The English word 'kingdom' is the one most often used to translate the Greek word 'basiliea', which means royal reign, rule, or territory subject to the rule of a king. It is a word that combines 'king' and 'dom' – the latter means state, or governance, or justice. 'Basiliea' is also sometimes translated as 'dominion', which is also the English word used for rule in Genesis 1. The 'dom' of dominion (and domain) comes from a Latin word meaning house. The two 'doms' of kingdom and dominion may actually have different root meanings in English, but this can be quite a helpful way of us understanding the kingdom of God and the temple of God. Each forms a 'dome' over us. The Kingdom 'dome' is the rule of God and the temple 'dome' is the house of God.

And it stands to reason that wherever God is dwelling, it's from there that he rules.[198]

The word 'temple' that we read about in the Old Testament is not actually a special religious word. It is simply 'house'. The word tabernacle is not religious either. It just means dwelling. There are sometimes words used for special areas that we translate as temple, but again these areas could equally apply to a palace. So where does God 'live' or 'dwell' and from where does he rule?

The psalms declare that God's throne is in heaven and there he is in his temple.[199] He has established his throne in the heavens.[200] These psalms are as much about God's presence with people on earth as a description of the sky or the spiritual reality where God's will is done. This takes us back to our understanding that God rules both in heavenly places and earthly places. The two are separated but only so that they can join together in willing mutual love and affection. This would have to be the case if God has made the universe based on love. His creation would have to have the chance to call out to him in a song of beckoning love. This is also poetically described in an erotic way in the Song of Solomon, which reveals how our sexuality reflects the surprising intimacy, love and connection between God and people.

The prophet poet Isaiah describes the difference between heaven and earth and also shows that they are connected by the presence of God. Of course, there is no place to contain God on the earth, except that his eyes are drawn

---

198. See: Boyd, Greg. Present Perfect: Finding God in the Now. Michigan: Zondervan, 2010.
199. Psalm 11:4.
200. Psalm 103:19.

towards Kingdom-hearted people. If there is anywhere he feels at home, it is in hearts and communities of humility and generosity.

> *Thus says the Lord,*
> *"Heaven is My throne and the earth is My footstool.*
> *Where then is a house you could build for Me?*
> *And where is a place that I may rest?*
> *"For My hand made all these things,*
> *Thus all these things came into being," declares the Lord.*
> *"But to this one I will look,*
> *To him who is humble and contrite of spirit, and who*
> *trembles at My word.[201]*

In Genesis 1 we saw that rule over the earth and its creatures was given to mankind. In the following chapter, this rule is exercised in the garden, with a view to being extended beyond the garden territory and filling the earth. In chapter 1, it is such a cosmic picture that it is hard to place where God is. He is there, before it all, then addressing it all: somehow very involved but also distinct – even in such a way that he can hand over rule to mankind. In chapter 2, God is intimately present – breathing into Adam, and then meeting with Adam and Eve in the garden in the cool of the day. The garden is his dwelling place on the earth.

The paradise garden is a place of rest. Gardens like this are very restful today: the running water, the shade, the fruit, the pathways. The order that has been brought through cultivating and protecting means that you do not feel the need to anxiously sort things out. The gardening work in a paradise is all good stuff for human beings. It is

---

201. Isaiah 66.

not surprising then that this is the place where God lives in the seventh day of his 'rest'. Where God is, there is rest. Noah was born to bring rest to an anxiety-filled creation and his ark was that place of shelter from the storm. In the same way, Solomon was born to bring rest and living in the temple was God's gift of rest to Israel.[202] And now, in an anxious world, the gift of the Kingdom of Heaven is the rest that comes from Shalom. Many of us feel most at rest in our own home. It is where we finally relax. Even after a holiday, it is often very comforting to be in your own home once again. The Kingdom is about being 'at home' with ourselves, our neighbours and with God. The garden paradise is the first example of this and so it is God's home on the earth.

The story of God among people develops as they invite him into their homes. Abraham and Sarah entertain angels who later leave but somehow the Lord remains there in conversation. Jacob meets with God and calls that place Bethel – the house of God. When the family is extended to become tribes, then God lives among them in a tent, like one of them, called the tabernacle. His presence is experienced in the Ark of the Covenant, and wherever that goes so His Shalom rule breaks out and overflows. Solomon's temple is a house given to God, in some ways similar to Simon Peter's desire to put up a tent for Jesus, Moses and Elijah: a way for people to physically and symbolically grasp that there is a God who is faithful and close. Ultimately it is prophesied that God will rule in Jerusalem.[203] God's throne and Jesus' ruling of a kingdom become more entwined as the rule of God is once again done through an Adam figure. Ezekiel

---

202. Genesis 5:29, 1 Chronicles 22:9, 1 Chronicles 23:25.
203. Isaiah 24:23.

sees a man on the throne. Jesus says He will sit on the throne. In the Book of Hebrews, Jesus is at the right hand of the throne of God. In Revelation the lamb is near the throne, on the throne and sharing the throne with God until there is no temple; the city itself is a temple and there is no difference between the heavenly throne and the earthly footstool. "And I heard a loud voice from the throne, saying, 'Behold, the tabernacle of God is among men, and He will dwell among them, and they shall be His people, and God Himself will be among them.'"[204]

The home then is central to the Kingdom of Heaven. The Kingdom is not just some huge edifice of an empire, where people vie for office along corridors of power. The Kingdom of God is the rule he has over his household. This is why, from the garden onwards, the home of the family and homes of the family of families are so central. In the New Testament, the new family model called the church is essentially a home or a household, a community. If the Kingdom of Heaven is the reign over a household, we don't get so caught up in images of diplomacy, taxes, statutes and bureaucracy. The reign is about when to eat together, use of the bathroom, planning holidays, having fun and playing games. In a household, there is still the need for rule, but at its best this is done through covenant agreements, loving negotiation and the honouring of gifts and skills.

My household has two young adults, my wife and I, and my mother-in-law, and a cat that the three of us are allergic to. A recipe for inter-generational/species disaster, you may think. In fact, the covenant we have means that

---

204. Revelation 21:3.

all the ironing gets done, 1970s English non-spicy meat-based food is frequently cooked, the sinks are bleached. Suspicions are roused that one partner in the covenant is doing all the work, while the others are sitting under the fig tree with their neighbours . . . In fact, the agreements of love and honesty mean that whether the food is spicy or plain, the heating is on high all the time or prudently turned down, the adult male is giving everyone lifts in the car or they are finally using their own initiative: it all works really well. (Thanks in part to inhalers and eczema cream!)

Home is where the Kingdom of Heaven is modelled through Abraham's family (hilariously or even comfortingly badly at times) and then through various other families that are focussed on, like King David's. What is in view is the role of the head of the household, how the rest of the family work out their mutual relationships and how others on the outside are treated, cared for and invited in to the family. This was the pattern in the garden, as Adam and Eve relate with God, love one another and care for their immediate environment then reach out towards Eden and the wider world. It is the pattern for Israel once it becomes a wider family. Most of the Pentateuch is about how Israel will relate to its Father, the Creator God, how they will get on with one another, and how they can influence and bring blessing to every other family tribe and nation on the earth.

The statutes and laws are essentially the ethos of God's household and the beginnings of the possibility of repeated patterns that will become a culture of the Kingdom of Heaven. The temple is also a blueprint for this ethos. It is not meant to be a railway siding into religion. Rather it is an image for us of the Kingdom Household of God. And as 'temple' actually most often means house, we see that the Garden of Eden is like a temple in its design. In fact, it is the pattern for the tabernacle of the Exodus and then the temple of Israel.

Selah, pause, reflect

What's your best experience of a household, a well-led home, a domestic experience that really worked?

What made it so good – the fun, security, food, chat, organisation?

Could you replicate it somehow? Is it worth making this our main ambition beyond career and wealth?

Grand designs

Eden was a paradise garden, designed and constructed by God. Once made, he invited man immediately into the task of naming and assessing what was there with a command to extend out this design and build into the earth. The emphasis is on rest and work, relationship and love. The tabernacle was similarly built, this time in a partnership between God and people, using beautiful materials and the skills of mankind being joined or augmented with the skill of God. It was temporary, and shifted with the movements of the people. This emphasised the nature of how we partner with God – we join with Him in where he is and what he is doing rather than necessarily expecting him always to come to us.

The temple was likewise designed and constructed, this time using not only the skills of the family, but inviting others, "aliens and strangers", to give generously and participate in the task.[205] This time it was situated on a mountain. This emphasised the heavenly nature of God's rule: the rejoining of the high-up heavens with the low-down earth. Not an attempt by people to scramble up there somehow, like the tower of Babel, but the gift of God to find a place midway between heaven and earth: up in the air but rooted in rock. The geography and settings of these various temple places combine together in showing us how purposeful God has been in working out His Kingdom of Heaven strategy.

When Jesus announced the Kingdom rule of God on the earth, of heaven coming close, he brings with him the

---

205. 1 Peter 2:11, 1 Chronicles 22:2.

peace and rest of the paradise garden. He is led into a wilderness without any raw materials to hone and fashion into the beauty of a tabernacle. His resources of trust and humility mean that his dependency is on God rather than his own skill and power. Then, wherever he walks, he is the fire and cloud of God, moving among people and bringing the same healing and justice that was at the heart of Moses' tabernacle. He clears out the Jerusalem temple so that anyone can get in regardless of race, place or circumstance. He is intensely glimpsed in a transfigured heaven-and-earth way in a temple of God's presence on a mountain, and humiliatingly stared at hanging on a cross as all the Old Testament sacrifices are stewed and burned in the one charred, bloodied and broken pot of his body. It is in a garden that he takes the full anxiety and pressure of the world on his shoulders and it is into a garden that he walks resurrected, like a new Adam. His presence and face are, at first, not recognised as he walks there, this time at the beginning rather than the cool of the day; where everything seems the same, but everything has changed. So finally the garden and city and mountain tabernacle-temple are all found together as the New Jerusalem, home to God and man, coming down from heaven so that Jesus and his family can rule and reign together.

The layout of the well-known wilderness tabernacle has at its heart the Holy of Holies. This is where the presence of God is most intense. This area is situated in the Holy Place, where the priests come and go. Surrounding this is the courtyard, into which the people of Israel come. And in the temple design, there is an outer courtyard with a door to the East, which is for all those who are beyond the family of Israel but who want to become a part of its culture.

Similarly, the paradise garden had in its midst the tree of life, where God walked in the cool of the day. The boundaried garden was the place where Adam and Eve were able to come and go freely. Eden was the immediate vicinity round the garden into which the family would multiply. Outside of Eden, to the east, was the rest of the earth's territory, to be subdued and ruled and filled.

This is the Kingdom plan all through the Bible. God turns up and his presence is remarkable and noticeable. He establishes a relationship with some people who begin to know him and serve him. His love asserts its rule in their hearts and relationships. This then spills out to those around them, running through family lines, business lines, cultural lines and establishing a wider ethos. As this Kingdom is then expressed among such a group of people and Shalom is worked out, experienced and enjoyed, so others looking on catch a glimpse of a great way of living and they too desire the Kingdom, even if their earthly culture and language appears different.

The tabernacle, then, is not just a random religious tent. Its purpose and design are a picture for us of how God continues to pursue his desire to rule and reign with mankind on the earth. Rather than relegating it to an outdated, albeit fascinating bit of worship history, it is a model for us that shows even when we are rootless, powerless and adrift, it is still possible to experience the ruling and reigning in the Kingdom of Heaven that is God's intention for us.

Priestly Patterns

Patterns of Walking

The walking and presence of God in the temple/tabernacle – God being intimate and among – reflects the walking and the presence of God in the garden.[206] God says to Moses, who is nervous about picking up the leadership mandate to subdue and to rule, "My presence shall walk with you and I will give you rest."[207] This is exactly what God did with Adam and Eve. He was present with them, walked with them and gave them his rest. It continues to be the desire of God for humanity. The same walking described in Genesis is used of God as he proclaims the Shalom Jubilee in Leviticus *26:*

So I will turn toward you and make you fruitful and multiply you, and I will confirm My covenant with you. You will eat the old supply and clear out the old because of the new. Moreover, I will make My dwelling among you, and My soul will not reject you. I will also walk among you and be your God, and you shall be My people. I am the Lord your God, who brought you out of the land of Egypt so that you would not be their slaves, and I broke the bars of your yoke and made you walk erect.

Jesus later walks around on the earth and invites people to join him in that walk. His walking on the beach in Galilee, recorded by Matthew, is the same walk of God in the

---

206. Deuteronomy 23:14, 2 Samuel 7:6.
207. Deuteronomy 31:8.

garden and in this Jubilee promise. Jesus invites people to follow him and promises that when they do, they will find rest for their souls.

Perhaps this is why pilgrimages are so deeply satisfying and increasingly popular. The rhythm of a walk, where progress that is made geographically enables an inner progress – in relationship with a companion, or quietly in our soul – in a way that sitting inert, or busily rushing cannot achieve. The pace of the stroll develops intimacy and trust, step by step, on shared pathways. Whether it is the road to Canterbury, the El Camino Santiago or the way to Jerusalem, the dwelling place of the King is not in a hole or a nest but in the challenge and reward of a jointly traversed journey.

Patterns of Speaking

The words "And God said . . ." and the seven times repeated "it was good" are echoed in the seven times "Yahweh spoke to Moses, and said . . ." for the creation of the tabernacle home of God.[208] God also declares that in this new work he is going to do some creating once more and that unique word to "create" is used again. And of course, both these series of 'God saying' end up with the work being completed – that is, Sabbath rest.

The words we say and the vocabulary we use create a culture. We can speak life and expect a culture of creativity, daring, compassion and justice, or we can tilt towards negative talk and construct a framework of fear, defensiveness and rivalry. This happens in a home, an office, a sports team or a social club. Words create and destroy. Six days of creation, August to May's football season, three months' new job probation

---

208. Exodus 25-31, Exodus 40:17-33, Leviticus 8.

or eighteen years of raising a child. A house can be blown down with a huff and a puff. The Kingdom of Heaven is not made out of nice words, pastel shaded rhymes and inoffensive suggestions, it is established on words that build, strengthen and give courage.

Patterns in Design

The Kingdom commands to Adam, to cultivate and protect, are exactly the same commands given to the priests in their work of serving and keeping in the tabernacle.[209] This is a kind of recreation. The trees and the flowers and the fruits of the garden, and the animals of the wider creation, are literally woven into the fabric of the tabernacle and temple which, along with the priests clothing, are decorated with these designs.[210] In the Holy of Holies is Aaron's budding almond rod, a representation of the tree of life in the middle of the garden. The cherubim are depicted in the Holy of Holies, in the same way that they guard the gate to the garden and the tree of life after the corruption of the garden home.[211] The precious stones mentioned in the rivers are then built in to the priest's clothing and the rivers themselves are observed in Ezekiel's and John's Temple visions.[212] The historian Josephus commented about the tabernacle design: "for if anyone do but consider the fabric of the tabernacle, and take a view of the garments of the high priest, and of those vessels which we make use of in our sacred ministration, he will find . . . they were every one made in a way of imitation and representation of the universe".[213]

209. Numbers 3:7.8.
210. Exodus 28, 1 Kings 6-7, 2 Chronicles 3.
211. Numbers 17:8, Hebrews 9:4.
212. Exodus 28:17-20, Ezekiel 28:13, Ezekiel 47, Revelation 22:1.
213. Flavius, Josephus and William Whiston. *The Genuine Works of Flavius Josephus, the Jewish Historian*. South Carolina: Nabu Press, 2012.

The Bible demonstrates that God is interested in clothes and their design and meaning. The same goes for interiors. In fact, it would seem that his artist nature has the same drives as our own, to create spaces and objects and garments that reflect who we are and what we believe. The 'house' – whether it is a fashion house, a product design house, a perfume house, a publishing house – is the domain of the artisan. So, an arts movement or design movement gives us an idea of the 'Kingdom movement' of God. A thread of values, belief, understanding of materials, work and appreciation that begin in a 'house' but end up influencing generations and cultures.

Pattern and Place

Solomon's temple has a similar design and function to the tabernacle, and therefore the garden of Eden. Ezekiel and Isaiah call Eden "the Garden of the Lord" and say that Eden is "the holy mountain of God", a reference to God's temple, as mountains and high places are those places where heaven and earth meet.[214] Bethel, the house of God where the ladder to heaven was seen by Jacob, is situated high up in the hill country. Solomon's temple is on mount Zion, Jerusalem, the heart of the Kingdom, and is the pattern for the household of God and therefore the family of Israel.

Place is inherently meaningful to us. Holy places are liminal. Where the earth and sky meet on a mountain. Where the ocean meets the land on the coast. Where night sky and desert join in their vastness. Wherever we sense a threshold, our spirits tend to unfold in awe and wonder.

---

214. Isaiah 51:3, Ezekiel 28:13.

It is in these places that God's promises and blessings are often made in the Bible. Equally the temple of the Kingdom of Heaven can be found in the melee of the city. Crowds of people are not always a sea of chaos but inspire the beginning of God-worship in their energy and variety. And even though there is a sea of people in malls, airports, sports stadia and concert venues, the Holy Spirit has the capacity to hover, stir and bring moments of mysterious glory; a carnival of praise in the 21st century city.

Fascination and Pattern

In a similar way to Adam's first ruling task to name the animals, King Solomon, a new Adam-King, like a Victorian botanist describes plant life from the cedar to the hyssop and animals and birds and creeping things and fish.[215] Solomon rules with order and wisdom and justice over the Kingdom because God is at home in his house, the temple. The temple is a new Garden of Eden, a new start for good rule on the earth after the corruption and decay of selfish violence. In fact, that terrible phrase "that every imagination of the thoughts of his heart was only evil continually", summing up the anti-Kingdom, is turned around by David as he plans this temple be a new direction for humanity.[216] He prays that "the imaginations and thoughts of their hearts," rather than being evil continually, might be "directed towards thee".[217] And where in Genesis 6 "God was grieved in his heart" over the rebellion, in the last book written in the Old Testament, Chronicles, it says of God and the temple that "His heart will be there continually".[218]

---

215. 1 Kings 4:29-34.
216. Genesis 6:5.
217. 1 Chronicles 29:18.
218. 2 Chronicles 7:16.

Extreme and evil religious devotion ends up locking down music, the arts and education. And yet Solomon represents beauty, wisdom, research, exploration and the arts. That is why the best priests are scientists, writers, mathematicians and those who love the earth as well as heaven, and the best religion serves widows and orphans with a reimagining of how the planet can be shaped. It takes imagination to solve problems and turn knowledge and wisdom into understanding. Priestly-ness is not simply fulfilling pastoral or religious duties, but the opening of the kind of imaginative thinking that happens deeply in our hearts.

Pattern of Government

The tabernacle and temple are depictions for us of the home of God where he will exercise his rule. The temple is of course a place of religious devotion – it has the altar, the priesthood, and the function of atonement. Nevertheless it is also the place of kingship and the function of governance. In the Holy of Holies is the Ark of the Covenant. This is really God's throne on the earth. It is also called the mercy seat – quite the opposite in nature to the throne of a despot or emperor. The heart of God's rule is mercy, a covering over of all that is corrupt, a seal against corrosion and destruction. When the Ark was 'lost' for a while, it brought fruitfulness and multiplication to whoever was near it. This is because flourishing is God's plan for people. In this case it was a farmer called Obed Edom whose land and property flourished while the Ark of the Covenant was in one of his tractor sheds. Moses and Joshua, who sought to subdue and rule in Israel, found their resource for this by meeting with God in the tabernacle. King David had a tabernacle and was zealous to bring the Ark of the Covenant into Jerusalem so that his reigning could be done through the power and wisdom of God and not just through his own efforts. King Solomon "sat on the throne of the Lord", so he is in effect a vice regent, like Adam and Eve ruling with God and on God's behalf.[219]

There is no reason why local councils, town halls, government departments cannot be as heavenly as an oratory. There is sometimes the tendency to keep kingship apart from priesthood, but the Kingdom of Heaven locates generous rule in the place of humble devotion. Although this is different to Christendom, where world power is owned by ecclesiastical power (and vice versa), the Bible points towards congruence, partnership and mutual respect between that which appears secular and that which looks spiritually minded. What might the presence of God look like in a borough rather than a cathedral? What place is there for merciful rule where forgiveness and cleansing are the order of the day?

Global Pattern

The temple is also the place into which all the families of the earth are invited. It was built by someone outside of the family of Israel, Hiram Abi. Solomon's prayer in its dedication is that all the nations would come to it. Isaiah called it a house of prayer for all the nations. It was built to be for God's "fame and splendour in the sight of all nations" through the skilled craftsmanship of people from all kinds of backgrounds and cultures, so it is not surprising that in Revelation "the glory and honor of all the nations will be brought into it".[220]

219. 2 Chronicles 9:8.
220. 2 Chronicles 6:32-33, Isaiah 56:7, 1 Chronicles 22:5, Revelation 21:24-26.

Religious activity tends towards exclusivity and hyper-partisanship. A sign of the Kingdom is a temple filled with people from different cultures. Technology has always made this more possible, whether it is the technology of printing and communication, or measuring longitude and building ships. Centralised power and conformity leads to an anti-temple, a tower of babel that grasps at the stars rather than invites heaven. But multiethnic, cultural and linguistic expression can be nurtured and celebrated rather than being compounded into monolithic fortresses. The diversity and spread of Jesus-following faith is truly extraordinary. It has an exciting danger. There is not one conforming language of Latin, English, or Arabic. There is no unifying musical priestly garb or liturgical style. The exciting danger is in the fact that across cultural lines no-one is quite sure if everyone else is as pure and orthodox as they are. Our suspicions in the West are that those in the East or South don't use cutlery properly, or have a tendency to irrational emotion, or stray into heresy using all the wrong metaphors. Conversely a western Christian faith has a dubious history of empire, greed and individualism. The risks of non-conformity are the delights of the Kingdom carnival. In the New Testament, the theme of Priest and King is picked up to describe a new family community of those who are brought together through the shared culture of the Kingdom of Heaven as lived by Jesus:

And coming to Him as to a living stone which has been rejected by men, but is choice and precious in the sight of God, you also, as living stones, are being built up as a spiritual house for a holy priesthood, to offer up spiritual sacrifices acceptable to God through Jesus Christ. But you are a chosen race, A royal priesthood,

A holy nation, a people for God's own possession, so that you may proclaim the excellencies of Him who has called you out of darkness into His marvelous light; for you once were not a people, but now you are the people of God; you had not received mercy, but now you have received mercy. Beloved, I urge you as aliens and strangers to abstain from fleshly lusts which wage war against the soul. Keep your behavior excellent among the Gentiles, so that in the thing in which they slander you as evildoers, they may because of your good deeds, as they observe them, glorify God in the day of visitation.[221]

The Human Temple Pattern

Although the physical earth is of course God's home and throne, it is not just the place of the garden or of the temple building that is important. The temple is wherever the spirit of God is living. It could be someone's life and body; it could be a home or a school or a hospital; it could be a farm or a rich wetland estuary habitat; it could be a group of friends or a mixed bunch of misfits. The temple is not so much a place of religious worship as a household of life. A royal priesthood and a holy nation are two titles that mix up the sacred and the secular. There is not meant to be a divide in these activities or identities. The temple is a place made special because of the rule of Shalom and beauty being exercised by a community. And, even if this is surrounded by those who don't have this culture, then the excellent and good behaviour and deeds of the household – that is 'good' just like created things were called good by God in

---

221. 1 Peter 2.

Genesis 1 – will point the way to a Kingdom that works and brings peace to everyone.

Because Jesus is our High Priest, we do not need humans to do the sin cleansing spiritual work of priests for us. What is exciting about Jesus, who was priest and king and calls his followers into these roles too, is that his access to God's heavenly rule of wisdom and peace is a here and now possibility for us also. Whereas in the Old Testament there were just a few priests and only one high priest who could actually walk and talk with God, Jesus showed a human life that didn't require ritual washing, the wearing of special robes, the obsession with vast amounts of sticky animal blood, or even the massive diet of cooked red meat. But the gradual build up of the plaque of regret, disappointment, the saying of stupid hurtful things, the jealousies and the angers, all press us down to a life of dust and heavy heartedness. Having a priest to relieve us of whatever burdens we have is a big relief, but many of us don't have that luxury, or if it is offered it doesn't seem to fully relieve us. If, however I am a priest as well as a king, then it means that whenever my kingship has gone awry, my priestly-ness can get me back on track. I can walk freely in the garden in the presence of God and feel the warmth of his sun on my back and even on my face.

Priesthood is simply the continuation of serving and protecting God's paradise garden. It is not for a special few, nor is it a religious function. True priesthood is the keeping of a covenant relationship between God and the earth, or mankind and the earth, or man and woman, or God and mankind. It corresponds to the Kingship of subduing and ruling. Most of the ways in which we live as humans on the earth require both these functions of priest and king. One is not more holy than the other. Nor is one more effective or practical than the other. A CEO must rule diligently for the sake of her staff, shareholders and customers. This ruling, however, is often best mediated through her function as priest, as one who creates a culture of honour and creativity. The head office is a palace: full of those who will get the task done; but it is also a temple that is meant to influence, guide and refresh every regional office, franchise or dealership in the nation or beyond. William Steere, past president of Pfizer, said in a speech to his company, "The future leader will consider the "ceremonial" or "spiritual" responsibilities as a required and critical function of the Head of the Organization, not as a trivial function to be handled or delegated in any other person. Those culture leaders who do not acknowledge or handle effectively the questions of visibility and accessibility of the Upper Management will limit the openness of the culture and will limit their ability to lead through the knowledge and personal influence, forcing the leadership to be executed through the position or hierarchy."[222] To lead through shaping culture, as a priest as much as a king, creates community, traditions, celebrations and unity.

Patterns

The homes of God – in the paradise, in the tabernacle and in the temple – are not coincidences or randomly unconnected desperate attempts to cure the soiled earth. They are all patterns and drawings, representations of what

---

222. Hesselbein, Frances, Marshall Goldsmith and Richard Beckhard. The Leader of the Future: New Visions, Strategies and Practices for the Next Era. New Jersey: John Wiley & Sons, 1997.

has always been in God's imagination. The tabernacle was built according to a pattern or blueprint given to Moses by God. But, according to Hebrews, the tabernacle that was built is in itself a likeness of something else that is heavenly. Jesus is now the High Priest and King, sitting on a throne in a heavenly tabernacle.[223]

So, the temple and tabernacle are patterns, based on the Garden of Eden, of what the Kingdom can look like as it spreads across the earth.[224] They point towards an ultimate dwelling whose canopy will stretch across the heavens and the earth. This is the future dream, even if the family is surrounded by enemies from the anti-kingdom empire and if that empire's yeast has a habit of pervading the family itself. The priests are architects of this Kingdom culture, umpires who lay a hold of both God and man so that the family of families can thoroughly enjoy their feasts of multiplication.

---

223. Exodus 25:9, Hebrews 8:5, Hebrews 9:23.
224. See: Beale, G. K. *The Temple and the Church's Mission: A Biblical Theology of the Dwelling Place of God. Illinois: IVP Academic, 2004.*
See also: Mayhew, Ray. "In My Father's House – Using the Temple as A Paradigm to Advance the Church, Global Mission, and the Kingdom of God." Ray Mayhew Online. https://raymayhewonline.com/bible-safari/in-my-fathers-house-pt-1/ (accessed February 12, 2020).

Selah, pause, reflect

The Altar.

A broken A L T A R, Lord, thy fervant reares,
Made of a heart, and cemented with teares:
Whofe parts are as thy hand did frame;
No workmans tool hath touch'd the fame.
A H E A R T alone
Is fuch a ftone,
As nothing but
Thy pow'r doth cut.
Wherefore each part
Of my hard heart
Meets in this frame,
To praife thy name.
That if I chance to hold my peace,
Thefe ftones to praife thee may not ceafe.
O let thy blefled S A C R I F I C E be mine,
And fanctifie this A L T A R to be thine.

"The Altar" is a poem by 17th century poet George Herbert.[225] It is a pattern poem in a collection called *The Temple*.
What does it say for you?
Where can you see the pattern of Jesus in your world, or your own life?

---

225. Herbert, George. *The Temple: Sacred Poems and Private Ejaculations.* Cambridge University, 5th ed., 1638.

Prophets, palaces and
on-the-edge places

The prophets are architects, too. This time, though, they are those on the sidelines: thrown into the pot with energy and power to shake, surprise and provoke the Kingdom plan back into action when it has turned towards corruption and lifelessness. The prophets carry the DNA of creation's original life form. They are not simply reminders of God's intention in creating the heavens and the earth. Their words and creative actions have power – to cut off the sickness and plaque that threaten to dull and suffocate Kingdom of Heaven life, and to bring a spark that will awaken faith, hope and love in the image-of-God humans who are meant to be stewarding the earth towards its fulfilment. The word 'created' in the Genesis account is only really used of God in the Bible. It refers to that divine making – inventing a new idea out of new materials. Usually it is used in the past tense about the Creator and about what he has done in making the heavens and the earth. However, it is the prophet and the psalmist who show that some new creating is now happening. A new heaven and a new earth, a new Jerusalem for people with newly created hearts.[226] This is the promise of the prophet: that the one who can make something out of seemingly no materials can bring the same creative power to bear to people's hearts and to the whole of the heavens and the earth. Prophecy is not just some good ideas, some bad warnings or some pretty

226. Isaiah 65:17-18, Psalm 51:10.

poetry. It somehow has the same breath and word that made the first earth and heavens. And now it is the way that the new earth and heavens are coming into being. Look, I am making all things new, declares Jesus, the ultimate spirit-filled prophetic Word.

The major prophets in the Old Testament speak life from within the family systems of temple life that has missed its Kingdom calling, and from without, when surrounded by dominant empires of power and oppression. Isaiah sings of the beauty of Shalom and of the Servant King who will rule and reign as God intended. Jeremiah reveals the emptiness of religious systems that do not have heart love at their centre. Ezekiel, pulled away from Judah, has a vision of the Kingdom plan of God kept in the heavens, and he declares its resolute intent. Daniel rules on the earth as a human should but also sees the rule in spiritual places and how possible it is for the true human, the new Adam and Son of Man, to be King, fully, in every sphere of created life.

The prophets who live among the people also keep pointing the way to God's original kingdom plan for humanity. Their behaviour and words look especially bizarre against a backdrop of selfishness, faithlessness and poverty, just as Jesus the prophet, looked wild and mad in his miracles, his upside down teaching and his revolutionary lifestyle. The Kingdom doesn't look normal when abnormality has become the new way of doing things. The Kingdom of Heaven is offensive and a stumbling block, a laughable comedy that is unreal foolishness. Nevertheless, the prophets often end up in places of influence; in life or death situations; in domestic locations where their words and actions bring the goodness of the Kingdom despite sin, ignorance or faith.

The prophets Elijah and Elisha represent for us how we might live in a Kingdom of Heaven way, even when confronted with the violence of empire or the sadness of a corrupted earth. Their lives are utterly human and understandable to us but they are also symbolic of a subduing and ruling life that is possible for anyone who would like to be connected to the creator king.

Elijah is the breakthrough prophet. He prepares the way and faces full-on the power of empire in the form of Jezebel and Ahab. Similar to John the Baptist's face-off with Herod, Elijah struggles with the overwhelming forces of violence and pride. To make a stand for the Kingdom of Heaven is not always experienced by sitting under a fig tree. Because this Kingdom is contested and even Jesus was murdered by the opposition's force, it is not surprising that Elijah loses hope, even after experiencing victory. Nor is it surprising that John the Baptist, a new Elijah, began to question whether the Kingdom of Heaven was really at hand when faced with imprisonment, death and a shattering of his dreams. Nevertheless, the story of Elijah and then Elisha, just like the story of John the Baptist and then Jesus and his disciples, demonstrates that a Kingdom life can be lived well in the here and now. And this, immensely and victoriously, by individuals who are able – in Jesus' words – to repent and believe.

How to live as a prophet
without being wild and hairy

Elisha's life is local and somewhat contained. He is not a Daniel who rules half the world, nor is he a family man poet like Isaiah. He is simply a son of man, who decides to live in the power of the creative breath spirit of God. He is used by God to care for the poor and to speak with kings. Like Jesus, his name means salvation, and also like Jesus, the salvation he brings is in the context of everyday relationships and opportunities. Therefore, his life is a pattern for us of how we might live prophetically in a world that doesn't fully recognise the Kingdom of Heaven. He lives in the power of the Holy Spirit, like Jesus lived and like the disciples lived so fully after the day of Pentecost. This meant being directed by the Spirit to rule and reign in particular places and at particular times, as well as to serve and protect wherever he might find himself at work, at home or out in the community.

Like the first Eden family and then Abraham's family, Elisha makes sure that he is located near to the presence and the house of God. Even without being near the official temple, in a land that doesn't recognise such a priestly pattern, it is possible to live in God's presence and be at home with Him. In fact, Elisha's journeyings reflect the pattern of those patriarchs who have lived Kingdom lives before him. He goes from Gilgal where he cuts himself off from the slavery of a previous life, travels to Bethel, the house of God and the place of intimacy with Him, then to Jericho where Joshua learnt to walk by faith trusting in a kingdom he could not see, and on to the Jordan where baptism, death and resurrection lead to living in the promised land of the Kingdom of Heaven. This is the journey of anyone who wants to see the Kingdom – whether Nicodemus experiences this as being born again, or the rich young ruler is challenged to find it through risk. It is the pattern written about by Paul to the Philippians:

> But whatever things were gain to me, those things I have **counted as loss** for the sake of Christ. More than that, I count all things to be loss in view of the surpassing value of **knowing Christ Jesus my Lord**, for whom I have suffered the loss of all things, and count them but rubbish so that I may gain Christ, and may be found in Him, not having a righteousness of my own derived from the Law, but that which is **through faith in Christ**, the righteousness which comes from God on the basis of faith, that I may know Him and the **power of His resurrection** and the fellowship of His sufferings, being conformed to His death; in order that I may attain to the resurrection from the dead.[227]

When Jesus says, at the beginning of Mark's gospel, that the time has come, the Kingdom of Heaven is at hand, repent and believe the good news, it is this journey that he is referring to.[228] Not that we have to leap on a plane, or get circumcised and dipped in the Jordan, but as the Kingdom is not of this world, it can only be entered into and lived in fully through a change of perspective in the heart. Otherwise our appreciation quickly turns to addiction and

---

227. Philippians 3:7-11, emphasis added.
228. Mark 1:15.

our hunger and thirst becomes greed. Elisha's life is one full of appreciation, friendship; political power and daily life, but he manages to live lightly and strongly with an eye on the heavens as well as an eye on the earth.

In 2 Kings, the stories – of recipes gone wrong, running out of resources, breaking a neighbour's borrowed power tool, deep friendships that mean grief is shared – are all stories that we can easily relate to. In many ways Elisha lives a normal, everyday life and faces the typical challenges that we each confront. In the midst of this, he does end up living in a universe where the usual laws are broken at times. Not so much that he can't enjoy that swim without hitting his head on the hard water, but enough that an axe head can float yet an enemy soldier can submerge and be healed. Salt thrown into a poisoned stream, flour thrown into a poisoned pot and a stick thrown into a greedy river all show that Elisha lived a life of effort and stretch as well as miraculous moments. There is a pressure that is needed when ruling. It is not a magical snap of the fingers. Even Adam's managing of the jungle took effort and creativity – it was a hands-on garden-creating project. Similarly, Elisha held in his hand the elements of the earth in order to throw them at the problems he was facing. He subdued the pain, desperation, grief and loss by ruling over what appears natural and also what appears supernatural. In Elisha's life it is hard to see the join between these things. He doesn't appear to be otherworldly holy; in fact, he lives with people and enjoys household life. But where the threat of death comes close, he seems to be able to grasp the Kingdom of Heaven with both hands and forcefully pull it into his surroundings.[229]

---

229. See 2 Kings 2-13 for these stories.

The twentieth century was an auditorium for a number of high profile prophetic voices. In the United States of America, Martin Luther King Jr. gave his voice to the plight of the African American people. Like Elisha, he felt a call that actually and physically moved him: "Just as the prophets of the eighth century B.C. left their villages and carried their "thus saith the Lord" far beyond the boundaries of their home towns . . . so am I compelled to carry the gospel of freedom beyond my own home town."[230] His existence was lived between the imaginative dream and the heat of the concrete and the power of the water hose. A prophet like King is known for the truthful beauty of his rhetoric. But this had resonance because he, and his Baptist Minister friends were also seen to be covered in the spit and dust of resistance. They chose to be extremists: "Was not Amos an extremist for justice: "Let justice roll down like waters and righteousness like an ever flowing stream . . . Jesus Christ, was an extremist for love, truth and goodness, and thereby rose above his environment. Perhaps the South, the nation and the world are in dire need of creative extremists."[231]

Elisha shows us that ruling in the Kingdom of Heaven is not a removed palace existence, but is all about engaging with the stuff of creation. Jesus, too, when doing his miracles uses spit and earth, breaks oily fish with his fingers, holds the corpse by the hand and tenderly touches the skin of the leper. Both these men live at the liminal intersection between the heavens and the earth. Elisha finds that his faith moves him to stretch himself out on the body of a dead boy – hand to hand, mouth to mouth. This is such a physical miracle. He is praying, which appears to be a

230. King, Martin Luther. *Letter from a Birmingham Jail.* London: Penguin Classics, 2018.
231. Ibid.

spiritual activity, and he is stretching, which is hard physical labour. It's then not easy to see how the boy comes to life – through one activity, or both? Jesus has power flowing from him – he speaks to a dead child, to Lazarus and from a distance to an enemy's slave. But such power does not prevent him from intimacy of touch or the sooty lighting of a barbeque without firelighter gel and a blowtorch. Elisha feeds one hundred men, Jesus five thousand. Elisha paces and prays, stretches and throws, Jesus commands calmly from the stern of the boat. There may be a difference in the scale of both men's ruling but the spirit is the same. Here are people who are committed to subduing the earth and having dominion, to restoring people's bodies and relationships.

Because the rule of empire will seek to crush enemy people and strip them of their culture, Elisha's Kingdom of Heaven activity inevitably ends up annoying the kings because of its pure justice and upside-down rewards. When the King of Aram wises up to the fact that Elisha keeps thwarting his plans to attack Israel, he sends an army to capture Elisha and his servant. This is another episode where the heavens and the earth are seen to connect and collide. Repenting is essentially seeing in a new way; it is having a Kingdom of Heaven perspective. The servant suddenly 'sees', like Daniel, that there is a spiritual order to this Kingdom as well as an earthly order. (It is what the high priest, ironically, does not see when questioning Jesus before his death: The Son of Man coming on the clouds with glory is the same Son of Man coming in to Jerusalem on a donkey; this King is ruler of the heavens and the earth.) The Aramean army end up blinded, not with their eyes opened; the fate of those who don't believe in the Son of Man according to Jesus in John 9. And because Elisha knows that the Kingdom of Heaven is not simply might is right, but is a Kingdom of Shalom, he brings the captured army to the King of Israel not to kill them but to be kind to them. The King of Israel leaps up and down wanting to slaughter them. Elisha tells him to spread a table before his enemies and let them feast. This story, with its espionage, anger, threat, heavenly vision, desire for revenge and comedic ending sums up the complexity and simplicity of the Kingdom of Heaven.[232] In the midst of a context that is compromised and emotionally charged, eyes that see are blinded and eyes that are blind are opened to freedom and feasting.

The apostle Paul writes:

> And even if our gospel is veiled, it is veiled to those who are perishing, in whose case the god of this world has blinded the minds of the unbelieving so that they might not see the light of the gospel of the glory of Christ, who is the image of God. For we do not preach ourselves but Christ Jesus as Lord, and ourselves as your bondservants for Jesus' sake. For God, who said, "Light shall shine out of darkness," is the One who has shone in our hearts to give the Light of the knowledge of the glory of God in the face of Christ. But we have this treasure in earthen vessels, so that the surpassing greatness of the power will be of God and not from ourselves; we are afflicted in every way, but not crushed; perplexed, but not despairing; persecuted, but not forsaken; struck down, but not destroyed; always carrying about in the body the dying of Jesus, so that the life of Jesus also may be manifested in our body.

232. 2 Kings 6:8-23.

For we who live are constantly being delivered over to death for Jesus' sake, so that the life of Jesus also may be manifested in our mortal flesh.[233]

Even under pressure, Elisha finds that he can bring the rule of heaven to release his enemies, his king and his servant into repentance; a new way of thinking. Jesus does the same in John 8. He too is surrounded by enemies, a mob of men who bring in a woman to be stoned. The temptation is to take sides with the mob or with the woman; to appease the law, the people or the Roman authorities. He takes people's eyes off the locked down impossible conflict and onto himself and his creative subduing of the dust of the ground. This is a supremely prophetic act. At this moment, everyone finds themselves once more in the hands of the heaven and earth Creator, who is able to judge and define and separate what has become fused and dirtily amalgamated. Like Elisha, Jesus opens the eyes of everyone there, so that the mob are set free to be individuals, the crowd are not forced into a brutally binary decision and the woman is allowed to see how she can live free from sin.[234] The story of the Aramean army is concluded in this way: "So he prepared a great feast for them; and when they had eaten and drunk he sent them away, and they went to their master. And the marauding bands of Arameans did not come again into the land of Israel."[235] Looks like the Kingdom of Shalom! Paul sums up Romans 12 with "Do not be overcome by evil, but overcome evil with good."[236]

---

233. 2 Corinthians 4.
234. John 8:1-11.
235. 2 Kings 6:23.
236. Romans 12:21.

As well as Elisha's commitment to friends and family, his calling embraces the political and the powerful. He does not ignore the politics of his day in order to seek quietude and solace away from a world that is too complex to engage with. The prophetic call is to engage fully with the world, even when it is not as we would like it to be. We have seen how Daniel fulfils this call and positions himself on behalf of the King of Heaven even as he works for the Kings of Babylon and Persia. Probably a major reason why our understanding of the Kingdom has become identified with the life of the church or with a future existence, is the difficulty we have in working out how we might live for the Kingdom of Heaven's values and purpose in a world that seems so opposed to these heavenly ways. Jesus shows us how these two kingdoms clash and how much conflict there is in both the heavenly spheres and the earthly realm. The violence and the screaming of the kicked out demon is proof that living in between the two ages is not all about saunas and massages, or even choir practice and village fetes.

Elisha is given access into the corridors of power. This is not so that he can build a safe career. In fact, he appears to annoy his political leaders as much as please them. But ruling and reigning as God's ambassadors is as much about being immersed in the worlds of commerce, industry, politics and the arts as it is in prayer and contemplation. The prophet Daniel is a great example of someone who did both in full measure. Isaiah, too, was a political adviser and therefore understood and lived in the complex machinations of the court. Elisha found that he had the respect of Kings. In fact, three Kings join forces in coming to him asking for advice and insight in 2 Kings 3. Elisha works for them but is also differentiated from them. He is in the system and yet his authority is not based on the whim of his bosses. In fact, his response in this story is cool and oblique. Like David before him, it is through music that he finds peace, wisdom and inner strength, rather than the charged chanting of the leader's rally. In another story, the enemy king is so desperate for his chief general to be healed that he writes a letter to the King of Israel. Like a TV drama, this is seen as a threat by the Israelite King who then typically offloads the responsibility to another – Elisha. And even the man to be healed gets angry with Elisha at being told to wash in a filthy enemy river.[237] Living prophetically for the Kingdom of Heaven opens all kinds of doors and makes unusual connections. The alliances that are made, however, are not done through bargaining and threat, but are fragile in worldly terms and rely on humility and faithfulness. Elisha also ends up being blamed for famine and disaster, even though he has worked successfully for the equivalent of MI5. His handling of power in God's Kingdom brings incredible breakthroughs, however, to individuals, armies and nations. The healing of Naaman, the enemy general, opens up this man's heart to a life of integrity and awareness of Elisha's God of grace. The truth that continues to be spoken by Elisha and the generous releasing of others to their destiny eventually leads to evil dynasties being destroyed, to a woman's land being restored through royal pardon, and to the prevention of two sons being sold into slavery.

The prophetic model is given to us in order to show us that we can live in an anti-Kingdom culture but still announce

---

237. 2 Kings 5:1-19.

the Kingdom of Heaven. We can mix with the powerful and the powerless without becoming disdainful or despondent. To live prophetically is to live as much in the future Shalom Kingdom as we do in present day creation groaning. The signs of the Kingdom breaking in will repel or attract. They may not bring the kind of affirmation and admiration we personally long for when we attempt good things. Such signs may, however, break open locked rooms and political strongholds so that the good and perfect will of the Father Creator is surprisingly and refreshingly experienced by friend and foe alike. For those who hunger and thirst for righteousness, they will be satisfied by the prophet's words and actions. For those who are dismayed that grace means blessing for every family of the earth and not just a chosen few, then sadly 20 or 30 pieces of silver is a small price to pay to silence the prophet.

Whatever reaction we provoke in people, there is a need for prophets to speak into the life of kings. Those kings today may have political power, or they may be men and women who are exercising their rule at home or at work. Although every human being has an innate sense of God's good Kingdom, the confusion that is caused by the prince of the air means this everyday rule ends up crushing, ignoring and excluding. Elisha's life shows how every king needs a prophetic voice. It shows how every community needs the wisdom and salvation of those who speak with imaginative authority and exercise power that is given by the Father creator. There is a role to play for every Kingdom-minded person that is all about opening people's eyes to the possibility that the Kingdom plan of God is available for them. To be a prophet is no more optional than to be a priest in the Kingdom of God. It is essential in these days where the Kingdom has still not fully arrived. Our challenge is to be free from an unhealthy fear of man and to be ready to stretch out our hands to heal. To have compassion that is more compelling than the admiration of others and to have eyes to see how God sees rather than to only see smallness, offence or impossibility. A bunch of prophets, living like Elisha will impact rich and poor alike. Living in between heaven and earth is unusually attractive to many people. The apostle Paul writes that such a life is not a cheap side show for pavement entertainment, but it is the fragrance of the garden city, the aroma that unlocks in people true memory and desire for life to the full:

> But thanks be to God, who always leads us in triumph in Christ, and manifests through us the sweet aroma of the knowledge of Him in every place. For we are a fragrance of Christ to God among those who are being saved and among those who are perishing; to the one an aroma from death to death, to the other an aroma from life to life. And who is adequate

for these things? For we are not like many, peddling the word of God, but as from sincerity, but as from God, we speak in Christ in the sight of God.[238]

Even in the midst of sorrow and exile, this is the purpose of the Kingdom of Heaven prophet.

---

238. 2 Corinthians 2:14-17.

Selah, pause, reflect

Where are you as a prophet? Close to power, and therefore sometimes envious of the lives that are led by those whom you are called to live prophetically for? Or on the margins of power, and therefore sometimes grumpy and disdainful of God's people and world?

Either way, reflect on these verses from Philippians 1 and let them shape who you are as God's provocative model for living well as a human:

And it is my prayer that your love may abound more and more, with knowledge and all discernment, so that you may approve what is excellent, and so be pure and blameless for the day of Christ, filled with the fruit of righteousness that comes through Jesus Christ, to the glory and praise of God.

Part 5

God-Pointing

'New' is the sign

There was a man of the Pharisee sect, Nicodemus, a prominent leader among the Jews. Late one night he visited Jesus and said, "Rabbi, we all know you're a teacher straight from God. No one could do all the God-pointing, God-revealing acts you do if God weren't in on it."
Jesus said, "You're absolutely right. Take it from me: Unless a person is born from above, it's not possible to see what I'm pointing to—to God's kingdom."[239]

This is a paraphrase of the beginning of Nicodemus' encounter with Jesus as told by John. Jesus is a sign and Jesus makes signs, and they all point towards the good news of His Kingdom. The phrase 'God-pointing' is a great summing up of Jesus the prophet, priest and king. He is always looking towards the Father, which then makes those around him follow his gaze. The gospel writer John builds his story around the signs of Jesus. The other writers describe his signs and wonders. Whether it is a rainbow or a baby in a manger, the whole Bible is full of signs. The literature of the Bible is often poetic or symbolic, to point us to the place where our minds are renewed so we can think with both our hearts and our minds. The histories are also replete with signs: Gilgal and the stones rolled over to make a monument, and the flesh cut into to make a permanent mark. The sign of the snake held up in the desert revealing healing. And the sign of the blood on the doorpost declaring freedom.

---

239. John 3.

Thomas Aquinas, in describing the sacraments, wrote, "the condition of human nature . . . is such that it has to be led by things corporeal and sensible to things spiritual and intelligible."[240] Of course, we understand the ways of a heavenly God by grasping hold of his imprint on the earth, but it is as true to say that we understand the reason for the earth and its created glory and fullness by finding its heavenly creator God and beginning a relationship with him in the cool of the day. The heavens reveal the glory of God; they point the way to his thinking and loving. The earth and heavens are his first revelation to us – before the word of God in the Bible and before we meet Jesus, the image of the invisible God.

God-pointing is the occupation of those who have tasted the Kingdom of Heaven and wish to know more. If the Kingdom of Heaven is the rule and reign of Shalom, then it is good news for everyone. Rather than keeping it a secret, those who have been touched by its generosity will do their best to paint it, sing it, machine it and dance it. The Kingdom is to be expressed – and if people won't do it, then the stones will begin to cry out.

In fact, people do express the Kingdom – every day. It is just that they don't always know they are doing it, and they are not always sure where the Kingdom ends and the anti-Kingdom starts. What begins as the Kingdom cry for freedom can end in a moan of sadness and we are not quite sure how we went from one to the other without noticing. Jesus is the perfect human being who always knows where the Kingdom is and where the anti-Kingdom lies in wait.

240. Aquinas, Thomas. *Summa Theologica*, Part III.61, 1271. Translated by the Fathers of the Dominican Province, New York: Benziger Bros., 1947.

He is proof that the true design of the heaven and earth can produce a human being who can rule well. Although Adam and Eve stepped out of the light of wise governing, and their sons and daughters followed suit, a new son of man has proved that the Kingdom of Heaven can exist fully on the earth. We have seen that this was not without battle and contest in his ministry, but his death and resurrection are the turning point for the Kingdom plan of God. It is no longer the case that the earth is irredeemable. If Jesus can come back from death, so can everything that was created by God, including the purpose to fill the earth and be fruitful.

When Jesus cries out "behold, I am making all things new", this is not a statement that has come to the conclusion that the first creation is no longer valid or worthwhile.[241] It is not a replacement new-making, it is more a restoring. It is the completing that was always going to happen. But now that things have become corrupted and Jesus died to save them, it is a completing that also purifies and makes whole. The Creation Kingdom plan always needed completing and fulfilling, not just by the human image bearers but also by God the father, giving place to His son to be its centrepiece and source. The declaration by Jesus now has chords of triumph and victory to add to that marriage consummation. If the Kingdom of Heaven were a new idea, however, that had nothing to do with God's original intention in creating the world, then it would be an option to discard the old earth and make an entirely and differently new one. The same could be said of people. Discard the old ones and start again with some new ones. But this is not how the Father of Creation sees humanity or the earth and the cosmos.

---

241. Revelation 21:5.

Because he loves what he has created, he wants it back, redeemed from the jaws of death and destruction rather than given a helping hand in that direction.

What kind of new is new?

The Bible is clear that Jesus rescues people. The transformation that comes through his rescue is also a making new. Somehow Jesus the separator and delineator and judge manages to destroy the old identity of sin and death and bring to life the new identity. The person stays the same but is different, now spiritually alive. In the same way, Jesus died physically in his body but then he came back to life with a new resurrected body, fit for both heaven and earth, bearing the scars of the old but engaging with reality in a new way.

Therefore if anyone is in Christ, he is a new creature; the old things passed away; behold, new things have come.[242] There is a newness to finding ourselves in Christ that happens even while still in a sin-corrupted body.

If any man's work is burned up, he will suffer loss; but he himself will be saved, yet so as through fire.[243] The baptism of fire that Jesus brings saves us by removing impurities. It also brings a passionate Pentecostal vigour that points to the Kingdom.

In the same way that people are made new in Christ, where the old has passed away and salvation comes by fire, so too the whole of creation will be saved and made new.

242. 2 Corinthians 5:17.
243. 1 Corinthians 3:15.

Peter writes about this in his second letter. He describes how the earth and heavens were first made out of waters in the beginning and then the earth was destroyed (literally, it perished) under water. However, its destiny is fire:

> But the day of the Lord will come like a thief, in which the heavens will pass away with a roar and the elements will be destroyed with intense heat, and the earth and its works will be burned up. Since all these things are to be destroyed in this way, what sort of people ought you to be in holy conduct and godliness, looking for and hastening the coming of the day of God, because of which the heavens will be destroyed by burning, and the elements will melt with intense heat! But according to His promise we are looking for new heavens and a new earth, in which righteousness dwells.[244]

At first this looks like a prophetic word that the creation will be entirely thrown out and not made new after all. Peter's vocabulary, however, is much like Paul's, who writes about people being saved and made new. In the same way that we see in our own lives that the "old things passed away", Peter says that the heavens will pass away. Just as any man's work is burned up and he is saved through fire, so too the earth and its works will be burned up and purified.

The destroying here is not the same as the 'perishing' through the flood or of ungodly men in verses 6 & 7, but it comes with the purifying fire and literally is a loosing and untying of ancient elemental bonds. The same word is used by John to describe Jesus' mission of loosing and setting

---

244. 2 Peter 3:10-13.

free – "to destroy the works of the devil".[245] Those elements are seen elsewhere by Paul as spiritual forces. Perhaps, too, the very elements of creation – the atoms and their constituent parts – that are groaning and crying out will be untied in this melting furnace of reckoning, redemption and release. Maybe there is a new physics at work here, or the refining revealing of the deepest physics that we are so desperately keen to know.

The new heavens and new earth we are looking for in verse 13 are similar to the new life we look for as individuals. The newness comes through the passionate fire of God, who redeems everything in all creation through the love of Jesus. Because I am now a new creation, so too can my earth become a new creation, and the heavens become a new creation. The end times are not the throwing away of beauty and creativity and the ecology of a wonderful planet, any more than they are the binning of a bunch of no hope people who God can't do anything with. The end times are times of renewal and passion, beginning as they do with the life of Jesus who declares that the future Kingdom is breaking in now, with all its heat-refined beauty and bondage-loosing power.

The new that is mentioned in the second letter of Peter, and in the Book of Revelation – for Jerusalem, the heavens and earth and indeed all things – is a fresh new, a renewed new, a new quality new, a reconciled changed back and changed up new. It is the old, now made new. It is the first creation genesis that is groaning to be made new. The Kingdom of Heaven that we look forward to is the fullness of

245. 1 John 3:8.

what the Kingdom of Heaven was always meant to be about. According to Peter, this is a place in which righteousness dwells. The new heavens and the new earth are not some brand new places, without continuity to what has gone before. The new me is not a different me that's never been thought of before, but me renewed, renovated, restored and now the person I was always meant to be.

This means that every person who finds new life in Christ is themselves a sign, God-pointing to a new kingdom that will embrace the whole of the cosmos. Jesus was the first sign, waking to new life on the first day of a new week. Having made everything in the first ever week, he is now making everything new as he meets with the women in the garden in the cool of the morning. One day God will fully dwell on the earth with mankind, but until then, Jesus, the complete human being, is God's perfect picture of the reign of the Kingdom of Heaven happening on the earth.

Selah, pause, reflect

What does it mean to live new, rather than try to be new?

When have you been surprised at being new? What has this felt like, how have others responded, has it become a pattern that is replicated and even spread more newness?

If creation becomes new in a similar way to a person, how does that affect your interaction with the earth?

The Son of Man is a God-Pointing Sign

The name that Jesus gives himself as the fulfilment of God's Kingdom plan for humanity is 'the Son of Man'. Jesus identifies fully with life on earth, even as the fully divine Son of God. This is because it is on humanity, rather than alligators or tulips, which heaven and earth wonder-and-fully rest: humans, with their likeness and image of God, but made from the same dust as the beauty of the earth. Jesus is the human of humans, a true Son of Man and Son of God, the rightful heir to the Kingdom. Jesus is a new Adam who can walk in the garden and not grasp equality with God, but instead, on the first day of the new creation week, point his friend Mary to His heavenly Father and include her and the disciples as his brothers and sisters in this new family.

Jesus refers to himself as the Son of Man over 80 times across all four gospels. This title is an interesting one as it is the one that God gives to his servant Ezekiel while God is referred to as "Lord God", in the same way He is known in Genesis 2 and 3 in the interactions he has with the first man, Adam. The Son of Man is inherently human, descended and distilled from the line of Adam. God is Lord God: the God of Gods and the God who is revealed to and known by humanity. The Book of Ezekiel is a wonderful partnership between this powerful and loving God and the obedient faith-filled dependent prophet. In this prophetic book, the Temple is redesigned and Israel, dry boned in the wilderness, is God-breathed once more, echoing the Word and Breath of God in the first creation days. *"I will put My Spirit within you and you will come to life, and I will place you on your own land."*[246] This becomes a direct promise about the Kingdom, with 'David' as King and God Himself dwelling in their midst. No need for temple, but instead a covenant of Shalom that governs the earth and heavens.

> *My servant David will be king over them, and they will all have one shepherd; and they will walk in My ordinances and keep My statutes and observe them. They will live on the land that I gave to Jacob My servant, in which your fathers lived; and they will live on it, they, and their sons and their sons' sons, forever; and David My servant will be their prince forever. I will make a covenant of peace with them; it will be an everlasting covenant with them. And I will place them and multiply them, and will set My sanctuary in their midst forever. My dwelling place also will be with them; and I will be their God, and they will be My people. And the nations will know that I am the Lord who sanctifies Israel, when My sanctuary is in their midst forever."*[247]

The sign of the Spirit breathing into people is a sign that the new King is now reigning and that God will come and fulfil what was first intended in the garden.

The Son of Man title that Jesus gives himself is also likely to be taken from the Book of Daniel. In chapter 7, Daniel sees Jesus the Son of God but calls him "One like a Son of Man":

> *I kept looking in the night visions,*
> *And behold, with the clouds of heaven One like a Son of Man was coming, And He came up to the Ancient of Days*

---

246. Ezekiel 37:14.
247. Ezekiel 37:24-28.

And was presented before Him.
And to Him was given dominion,
Glory and a kingdom,
That all the peoples, nations and men of every language
Might serve Him.
His dominion is an everlasting dominion
Which will not pass away;
And His kingdom is one
Which will not be destroyed.[248]

In an inversion of male and female being made in God's likeness, now Jesus, God himself, is 'like' a Son of Man. If people are made in God's image, then it is not surprising that he also is recognisable to us. As a Son of Man, Jesus is a new Adam and also a new Israel – he is descended not just from humanity, but from the line of those chosen by God to bring humankind into covenantal relationship. Jesus is God's servant Jacob, God's chosen King, David. This Son of Man is the heir to all the promises that have been made to the human race.

As he comes in the clouds, this Son of Man is like a priest, surrounded by the presence of God and bringing the presence of God wherever he goes. He comes up to the Ancient of Days, ascending as he did in clouds weeks after his resurrection, connecting earth to heaven. Then the language of Kingdom and rule is used once more (in imperial Babylonian Aramaic), and the serving and cultivating required by God of man to the earth in Genesis 2 is now directed towards Jesus the King as worship. Then, in verses 18, 22 and 27, Jesus – in characteristic generosity

---

248. Daniel 7:13-14.

and grace, fulfilling all righteousness spoken by God in Genesis 1 – now gives his rule and reign to the saints.

> *'Then the sovereignty, the dominion and the greatness of all the kingdoms under the whole heaven will be given to the people of the saints of the Highest One; His kingdom will be an everlasting kingdom, and all the dominions will serve and obey Him.'*[249]

Jesus, as the true Son of Man, is given all authority in heaven and in the earth. He is the sign of the Kingdom. His acknowledgement of this to the High Priest is what gets him handed over to the Roman Empire. Nevertheless, it is the recognition of Jesus, the Son of Man, that brings the power of the Kingdom of Heaven into lives and places all through history and round the world. He is the eye-opening 'Behold', and every other behold moment is a glimpse and image of Him.

For Daniel, the Kingdom is now fully manifest in this vision, a kingdom beyond even the great kingdoms he has served in his career. For Elisha's servant, the seeing of the hosts of heaven and then the enemy soldiers seeing of the banquet are also moments of a kingdom that is more powerful and more lovely than any imagined or experienced. Jesus was keen that people really saw him fully. From the High Priest who was about to have Jesus tortured, to John the Baptist who himself was about to be tortured, those who have eyes to see will see the King and His Kingdom in the small moments and in the great miracles. The Kingdom of Heaven has not been dormant since Genesis 3, nor is it only found in some narrow religious experiences. The Kingdom

---

249. Daniel 7:27.

of Heaven is the unfolding of God's eternal grace and power and it is close enough to touch and near enough to see.

Selah, pause, reflect

Allow these words of Jesus to open your imagination. What sense do they make in your current experience of living?

But immediately after the tribulation of those days the sun will be darkened, and the moon will not give its light, and the stars will fall from the sky, and the powers of the heavens will be shaken. And then the sign of the Son of Man will appear in the sky, and then all the tribes of the earth will mourn, and they will see the Son of Man coming on the clouds of the sky with power and great glory. And He will send forth His angels with a great trumpet and they will gather together His elect from the four winds, from one end of the sky to the other.

Now learn the parable from the fig tree: when its branch has already become tender and puts forth its leaves, you know that summer is near; so, you too, when you see all these things, recognize that He is near, right at the door. Truly I say to you, this generation will not pass away until all these things take place. Heaven and earth will pass away, but My words will not pass away.[250]

---

250. Matthew 24:29-35.

Kingdom Spotting

Discipleship is the art of spotting the Kingdom of Heaven. When we see the Kingdom, we will either be attracted or repelled. We are attracted because deep calls to deep. The image of God in us cries out with a groaning and a longing to express faith through love. Like the creatures in Hopkins' poem, we exult in how and who we have been made. We are repelled because the goodness of the Kingdom scandalises our de-formed nature. The grace of the Kingdom comforts and challenges us. Stepping into the Kingdom when we see its evidence is like a new birth and requires new thinking, language and movement from us. This is the walk of faith, walking round the brick walls of Jericho feeling the fear, but trusting in the love and victory of a God who breaks barriers, snaps chains and turns fortresses into garden cities of gladness.

When Jesus declares the Kingdom has arrived in Matthew's and Mark's gospels, he says that the way of handling it is to see differently, to have a change of mind, which is repentance.[251] This change of viewpoint leads to a life of faith, which is how we live in the Kingdom of Heaven now, even though it is still arriving and has not yet fully arrived. This is the same as Paul's prayer, that the eyes of our hearts would be opened to grasp the fullness of God's Shalom inheritance expressed through his love.[252]

---

251. Matthew 4:17, Mark 1:15.
252. Ephesians 1:18-23.

In John's gospel, in the story of the healing of the blind man in chapter 9, the fact of Jesus giving sight to the blind is evidence that the Kingdom is near. He does it through a reminder that God first subdued the dust of the earth and made human beings out of clay. The story is not simply about the physical sight that the man has received but about who can see and know what has happened. People around can't really 'see' what has happened — they're not sure it is the same man; they cannot believe this has happened. It is a story as much about what people know or don't know, what they believe or don't believe, as it is about the miracle of physical sight. Such is the Kingdom of Heaven: in its force and startling power there is inevitably a jolt, a shock, an earthquake tremor. The strangeness of it in a world that has become used to sadness, ignorance and impossibility causes people to stumble either into a newly-opened-eyes existence, or even into a hard-hearted refusal that anything could ever change. The previously blind man is asked by Jesus, "Do you believe in the Son of Man?"[253] With all we know of the Kingdom of Heaven, what a brilliantly simple and complex question!

So many of the encounters with God throughout the Bible are described in terms of seeing. (Ironically, this was the serpent tempter's suggestion in the garden paradise where revelation was already unfolding daily.[254] The suggestion was that by becoming rulers without God, Adam and Eve's eyes would be opened and they would be like God. In fact, their eyes are opened instead only to nakedness, shame and fear.) The new seeing that happens in visions, theophanies, dreams and meetings is a seeing of the

253. John 9:35.
254. Genesis 3:5.

Kingdom of Heaven, God dwelling on the earth. The word that crops up most is 'behold'. It appears to be a somewhat quaint and old-fashioned word used only in children's nativity plays. It sadly doesn't appear in some of the most widely read translations of the Bible but it is an exclamation of the Kingdom that can hardly be articulated, such is the surprise it echoes.

Behold!

Behold means 'See!' It is Archimedes' "Ahh" when sloshing water over the bathtub; it is the drum roll and cymbal of the magician's trick; the strident chords of music as the plot is revealed; the screaming giggle of the found child in hide and seek. This imperative command shouts to us to seize the moment, to grab it with both hands, to write down the vision and to make the most of the opportunity.

So, it is not surprising that Mark uses the word Kairos when he reports Jesus saying, "The time is fulfilled!"[255] Kairos means opportune, crisis, fulfilment, significant time. Kairos was a Greek god with very long hair who ran extremely fast. If he ever passed you by, then you had to grab him by the hair before you missed the moment. And this moment was luck, or favour or opportunity. 'Carpe diem' has a similar feel, as does the UK lottery phrase "It could be you", or the line "It's your lucky day". This is what favour feels like, favour being that Jubilee trumpet of a grace that is undeserved but freely available. The Kingdom of Heaven, full of goodness, kindness and the blessing of Shalom feels to us a bit like luck. It is not random, however, but has clearly had more planning

255. Mark 1:15.

and strategy than any scheme of man. God is certainly not capricious, but he does lavish his love. When this happens, and we glimpse with an intake of breath the relief and beauty of the God-pointed moment, then we feel like Joseph in Tyndale's translation of Genesis 39:2, "a lucky fellow".

Kairos moments of seeing heaven breaking in are also experienced when God passes people by. He passes by Moses and Elijah and is revealed in such an incredible way that they have to be hidden in rock clefts. They are transformed as heaven rushes by, close enough to touch, the very presence of God. The same word used for these moments in the Septuagint is used when Jesus passes by the disciples in the midst of their own storm. They are scared for their lives and see Jesus walking on the waves, and he is recorded as intending to "pass by them".[256] It is one of those bizarre and hilarious moments in the Bible: that Jesus would be hoping to simply stroll past, overtake on the inside with very little fuss and bother. But of course, this isn't what is meant by his passing by. It is the same coming close of the King that Moses and Elijah experienced in the midst of their own fiery storms. They must have got used to it, as they were ready to capture it on the mount of transfiguration when Jesus is revealed again so stunningly. But Peter was shocked and unable to contain himself and the disciples were afraid, able to see only an apparition rather than the full reality of the new Kingdom Son of Man ruling over the waves. At the end of these passings by, Moses bowed low to the earth and worshipped, Elijah stepped forward into his God-called life and the disciples were amazed, astounded and astonished.[257]

---

256. Mark 6:48.
257. Exodus 33:12-34, Exodus 10:1, Kings 19:9-21, Mark 6:45-52.

When we lift up our eyes and look, then there will be a moment of 'Behold' and we see clearly. This is a formula that is applied a few times in the Bible, especially to the patriarchs.[258] Abraham lifts up his eyes and looks and behold, he sees the three angels who bring him the promise of laughter that will accompany this first family of families. In agony and desolation, thinking that this laughing Isaac will be lost to him forever, he lifts up his eyes and looks, and behold he sees a ram caught in thorns – the provision of God. This formula is how Isaac's first encounter with Rebekah is described and then how Jacob meets his estranged brother Esau. Such are the significant kairos moments when the kingdom breaks in: for falling in love, for apology and forgiveness, for meeting with God's messengers and for being rescued by Jesus' act of sacrifice.

These kingdom glimpses are earthed in physical reality – the ram, the three men, the beautiful veiled girl – but they are signs of God's bigger Kingdom plan. The Kingdom of Heaven is shown in moments where this event, this experience, this activity, this love, is that which was prophesied and longed for, planned for before the world began. Abraham, Isaac and Jacob all seized these moments and believed in their reality and significance. They deliberately lifted up their eyes from the mundane and sadly impossible, to what might be happening in heavenly places. They actively looked rather than giving an unbelieving cursory glance. There was a 'moment', a 'behold' that they experienced with force and surprise. They saw. Something new was unfolding before them that was important and significant for them to grab a hold of if they chose. They were those

---

258. Genesis 18:2, Genesis 22:13, Genesis 24:63, Genesis 33:1. See also Daniel and Zechariah's visions.

who repented and changed their minds from unbelief to faith in the promise of God. Joshua, too, when faced with the fortress Jericho, lifted up his eyes, looked and 'behold', saw the Captain of the Heavenly Hosts. The in-breaking of the King caused the old enemy ground to become holy and heavenly, where anything is now possible and even ruler Joshua bows the knee and then sounds the trumpet. Peter seized the moment on the day of Pentecost and declared it loudly. A disciple is one who sees, recognises, seizes the 'This is That' moment and then God-points towards the Kingdom.

Most God-pointing actually takes place in everyday life. This is where the humble King is in evidence. It is in our actions of Shalom, in those upside-down blessed Kingdom behaviours. Every time we extend grace through the barrier of animosity, we point to the Kingdom. Every breath that we breathe that comes from the Spirit of God creates a new man out of the old. In this clouded nature of our lives, where we experience at the same time both the Kingdom of Heaven and the anti-kingdom, it takes courage and faith to not give up.

Look! There will be Shalom!

One of Elisha's closest friends, the woman known as the Shunammite, loses her son, whose birth had been miraculously prophesied by Elisha.[259] She stretches in faith and lays the dead boy on the prophet's bed. Her husband cannot see the connection between heaven and earth and only gets as far as a religious response. Perhaps it is

259. 2 Kings 4:8-37.

the vastness of the heavens that often means we become superstitious like this and revert to being at the mercy of fates and forces. On the one hand, religious rules give us some opportunities for favour if we play the ritual dice right. On the other hand, there are so many reasons why the alignment of the planets are never quite right, that we can become confidently and even comfortably powerless. The great thing about being without power is that we are clearly not to blame, and the feeling of not taking responsibility is like a drug-induced stupor. It is often men in the Bible, like Adam, Abraham and Jacob, who take the irresponsible option of faith not fate.

The Shunammite's statement is "it will be well", which literally means 'there will be Shalom'.[260] It is a belief in the original plan of God in the face of the worst that the Kingdom-robbed world throws at her. She runs out to meet Elisha. She decides to grab a hold of fate and wrestle it to the ground. Elisha has a moment of 'behold', but although he sees something, the reality for him is still clouded, he cannot quite make out what is wrong. He reaches towards her with tentative and uncertain Shalom hopes.

Once more her response is Shalom. Similar to the disciples guarding Jesus from the children, Gehazi, Elisha's servant, pushes the woman away. Shalom is often seen as childish and naïve; a distraction from the complex navigations of living in the anti-Kingdom without getting too bruised. But she is the one who has faith. She is like the Roman centurion and the Syrophoenician woman. She appears to be an outsider with no access to God, but her powerlessness and poverty of spirit is what grants her the inheritance of

---

260. 2 Kings 4:23.

the Kingdom demonstrated through her faith. In this story, Elisha extends himself in risky and embarrassing ways. Living between the ages is uncertain and exposing. It is a battle for the boy's life. Elisha turns out to not be Gandalf after all, and his staff sent to touch the dead boy is not even as powerful as a stick thrown in the river. (His servant, however, does turn out to have some Gollum about him in his desire for the power of riches rather than the riches of Kingdom power.) Instead Elisha faces death strongly, personally and intimately. He is bold and courageous and does not give up. Life breaks in but with no magic wand or spoken formula. It is more like prayer and pacing and perspiration. The only thing that counts, as ever, is faith expressing itself through love. The way we truly live is in touch with the Creator God, even if this is in the midst of confusion, misunderstanding or opposition. In fact, a God-pointing life is not one that is most often done in shining armour, on top of a victorious hill with strides of command and control. The Kingdom of Heaven is revealed in the smallest acts of kindness, sacrificial giving and daringly foolish steps onto wet and watery waves.

Selah, pause, reflect

Fill in the gaps . . .

What do you see?

Can you not see it?

Look!

I lifted up my eyes, looked, and behold I saw . . .

Spotting, judging and connecting

God-pointing also happens when we make Kingdom connections, when we spot where God is working. Jesus did this often when he met people. With Simon, Jesus spotted the destiny of being a rock and foundation. With Nathaniel, he spotted the heart of a true Israelite. With The Roman centurion and with the Syrophoenician woman, he spotted great faith. Jesus saw Zaccheus when no-one else did, and the woman with the issue of blood. He met the woman at the well, connecting her yearning heart to her true God, and he saw what was being reasoned in the hearts of the scribes and his own disciples. In all these cases and more, he does not make an angry judgement of these people, nor does he ignore their issues. As a faithful friend he speaks the uncomfortable but liberating truth and makes it possible for all these individuals to be connected to their heavenly father. God-pointing is the art of pointing out the blindingly obvious. Jesus said, "For judgment I came into this world, so that those who do not see may see, and that those who see may become blind."[261] This is the judgement that strips us of our conceit and says that the emperor isn't actually wearing clothes. It is the judgement that produces an "Ah!" and an "I see now!"

Judgement is one of those religious phrases that brings to mind judgemental people who have clearly eaten from the tree of the knowledge of good and evil and are more

---

261. John 9:39.

than happy to say so. But true judgement is really helpful. Although I pride myself in making great puddings, my lack of judgement with the ingredients doesn't always mean I get the results I want. I need to make the connection between the hardness of the cake and the invisibility of the words 'self-raising' on the bag of flour. This brings us back to the importance of our commission to rule. Judging helps us see what is true. A judgement brings release and clarity. The marked essay shows what has been understood and what still needs some work. The well-judged scalpel divides between tumour and health. The judgement of 'Not Guilty' to the innocent man must be incredibly liberating. When we are not sure of ourselves, our health, our motives or the impact we have on others, the making of connections and their resulting judgement brings much needed release. The apostle Paul knew the art of making these connections. He saw that Elymas was confused and confusing, not quite the Son of Jesus he claimed to be, and this judgement then freed the Proconsul of Cyprus, who was under Elymas' spell. Paul embraced the culture of Athens with all its provocative sickness and made the connection between the shrine to the unknown God, their poetic culture and the Creator of the heavens and earth. Jude, in his letter, shed new light on various writings and philosophy to hand, and John in the book of Revelation used the contemporary apocalyptic literary form to make the connection between the Empire of Rome, God's own Kingdom and the rulings that will go on to the end of the ages.[262]

---

262. Acts 13:6-12, Acts 17:16-31. See also Jude – 'Book of Enoch' and 'Testimony of Moses'.

We can make connections like this, too. We can observe what God is doing in people's lives, in communities and organisations. We can speak what we see and make it real through prophecy and encouragement. We can point to the hand of God, clear and present in culture and say This is That. We can agree with others about what we see in life and our world, putting words and phrases to commonly shared experiences that make sense to both head and heart. We can also speak in parables, like Jesus, so that the connection we make is oblique, yet intriguing, a mystery that encourages seeking and reflecting and waiting before the moment of Behold! The art of preaching is all about making connections, but so is consolation. A cup of water, or in the UK a cup of hot tea, opens up ears and eyes to receive grace and comfort. The signs of the Kingdom can be everyday familiarities or can be such stuff as dreams are made on. A relatively unschooled fisherman can boldly proclaim "This is what was spoken of through the prophet Joel",[263] as can the mystic John write that he saw "a river of the water of life, clear as crystal, clear as crystal coming from the throne of God and of the lamb".[264]

---

263. Acts 2:16.
264. Revelation 22:1.

Selah, pause, reflect

Righteousness and Justice are a pair of words that most often describe the nature of God's good rule.[265]

Why do righteousness and justice sometimes make us feel uncomfortable – to either give or receive them?

When have righteousness and justice brought release and freedom?

What connections and judgements do you need to make that will bring God's good rule to someone?

---

265. Righteousness and Justice are English words that often translate the Hebrew word 'tsadaq' which combines our understanding of rightness, straightness, and fairness, personally publicly and relationally.

Architects, artists and engineers of the new Kingdom culture

Artists, poets and musicians have been making connections for thousands of years. Aristotle's theatre brings catharsis: an audience can gasp in dismay and silently refuse to applause at the end because of the truth that has been experienced. Music and song somehow captures the essence of our existence. The stirring of memory and desire is how such culture grabs us and puts a mirror up to nature, and then, especially when the prophet is actively present, we can hear and share in the groaning of all creation waiting for its liberation into freedom and glory. An artist is prophetic, not just in the signs they use to point towards obscured realities but also in the way they subdue their material. They are in the image of God as they take words, sounds, colours and materials to form and fashion them into signs that have both form and meaning. The very act of subduing and ruling reflects the King's reign. This is why artistic production, which doesn't seem to have much utilitarian value, actually has such immense value, capturing as it does the spirit of humanity and therefore the God-breath that was first breathed into our nostrils.

God-pointing happens when colour, signs, design and language all expresses the nature of our complex and creative God. Artists make the invisible, visible. In this way, Jesus was an artist as he was the image of the invisible God, fleshing out the Word in bodily form. Jesus is the Light of the world, shining truth and glory. In the beginning, Father, Son and Holy Spirit create the world as artists; God's attributes, power and nature being clearly seen in and understood in what was made.[266] Engineers grasp a hold of invisible power and force, and by understanding and subduing the stuff of earth, this force is seen in what it generates and upholds. In Jesus all things hold together, and all things came into being through him. He is the chief cornerstone, builder and architect.[267] As those made in the image of God therefore, we too are artists and engineers who make connections and fashion the Kingdom culture around us. Erwin McManus in *An Unstoppable Force* helpfully describes an architect as both an artist and engineer.[268] Paul is an architect in this way, too – he says he is master builder laying a foundation on which to build the Kingdom city.[269] His work is to shine light on the mystery (of the Kingdom) that has been hidden for ages so that the manifold wisdom of God, Jesus and his character, might be revealed in the church, the people of God's Kingdom culture.[270]

Designing and building is right at the heart of the Kingdom of Heaven project: from the beginning where God was creating, forming and fashioning; in the garden that he designed and built; in the tabernacle and temple designs and constructions; in the life saving ark; and in the plans for vibrant street life. In the beginning, according to Proverbs 8, Jesus was not only Wisdom but constantly at God the Father's side, as a master builder, or architect. Every day, Jesus was the Father's delight, rejoicing before him,

---

266. Romans 1:20.
267. Ephesians 2:20, Hebrews 3:4, Hebrews 11:10.
268. McManus, Erwin Raphael. "Chapter 6: The Cultural Architect." *An Unstoppable Force: Daring to Become the Church God Had in Mind*. Colorado: David C Cook Publishing Company, 2013.
269. 1 Corinthians 3:10.
270. Ephesians 3:8-11.

rejoicing in the world, his earth and having his delight in the sons of men.[271]

Jesus loves being an architect. He loves building stuff with God and with people. It comes as no surprise then that his occupation on earth was a builder. This makes sense in the big picture and themes of the Kingdom. It also demonstrates that Jesus is humble enough and enjoys human experience enough to want to tidy and decorate, to solve problems and use power tools, to design and build a home fit for a leper or paralysed man, as well as a king. The Kingdom of Heaven, however, as its title reveals, is as much about the culture of faith, hope and love as it is about wattle and daub or beams and windows. Jesus may well have been involved in building the cities of Sepphoris and Tiberius but his major building project was to do with people. He said he would build his 'church', a community of active citizens joined together with truth and love.[272]

A cultural architect is one who technically and creatively designs a culture, bringing influence through ethos and then repeated symbols and patterns, eventually making behaviours natural and spontaneous. At the beginning of this century such a title was unheard of, apart from in McManus' book mentioned above and also by sports psychologist Willi Railo and England football manager Sven Goran Eriksson. Along with other sports scientists, their research and practice examined how certain athletes who are cultural architects "are people that are able to change the mind set of other people. They're able to break barriers, they have visions, they are self confident and they

---

271. Proverbs 8:30-31.
272. Matthew 16:18, Ephesians 4:15-16.

are able to transfer their own self confidence to a group of people".[273]

Jesus was a cultural architect in this way, creating a context of hope and delight by knowing deeply who he was, exercising self-control and serving those around. His signs and words gave common expression to his mission. King David, as poet and tactician, similarly was an architect of a culture that produced mighty men and insightful women, people who were loyal and kind, who exercised faith, wisdom and boldness. Cultural architects are those who produce mental clones on the pitch, who share the same mental model of commonly held values and strategies. "If you see a team with a shared mental model things will happen almost flawlessly. To see a situation and to, in a common fashion, read that situation and then to arrive without any conversation at a solution which is the same, so every-body's pulling, if you like, in the same direction, singing from the same hymn sheet."[274] The Kingdom of Heaven is established by men and women who live out disciplines of love in such a way that the atmosphere changes around them.

T. S. Eliot, reflecting on life at the beginning of the 20th century, wrote, "The dominant force in creating a common culture between peoples each of which has its own distinct culture, is religion . . . I am talking about the common tradition of Christianity which has made Europe what it is and about the common cultural elements which this common Christianity has brought with it . . . It is in

273. "The England Patient." BBC Two. https://www.bbc.co.uk/science/horizon/2001/englandpatienttrans.shtml (aired 23 May, 2002; accessed 13 February, 2020).
274. Ibid.

Christianity that our arts have developed; it is in Christianity that the laws of Europe have until recently been rooted. It is against a backdrop of Christianity that all our thought has significance. An individual European may not believe that the Christian faith is true, and yet what he says and makes and does will all spring out of his heritage of Christian culture and depend on that culture for its meaning."[275]

To make long lasting change where the Kingdom becomes our natural habitat, our world needs architects and influencers whose lives of signs – artistic and technical, natural and supernatural – will create a culture that reflects the house of God; one that says: this is that which was always planned, kept in heaven for you.

Selah, pause, reflect

In what ways are you a 'Maker'?

How does this identity and calling flow from the newness of life that is in you?

"You will be a sign to them and they will know that I am the Lord." [276]
Ezekiel lived out his signing – in vision, words, actions and lifestyle. In what ways have you been called to be a sign pointing to the Kingdom?

---

275. Eliot, T. S. Christianity and Culture. California: Harvest, 1977.
276. Ezekiel 24:27.

A Kingdom of Heaven Epithalamion

Psalm 45 is an Epithalamion: a poem written about the bride (and in this case the groom) It was written for a King's wedding but contains the language of the Kingdom of Heaven in its breadth, strength and beauty.

My heart overflows with a good theme;
I address my verses to the King;
My tongue is the pen of a ready writer.
You are fairer than the sons of men;
Grace is poured upon Your lips;
Therefore God has blessed You forever.
Gird Your sword on Your thigh, O Mighty One,
In Your splendor and Your majesty!
And in Your majesty ride on victoriously,
For the cause of truth and meekness and righteousness;
Let Your right hand teach You awesome things.
Your arrows are sharp;
The peoples fall under You;
Your arrows are in the heart of the King's enemies.
Your throne, O God, is forever and ever;
A scepter of uprightness is the scepter of Your kingdom.
You have loved righteousness and hated wickedness;
Therefore God, Your God, has anointed You
With the oil of joy above Your fellows.
All Your garments are fragrant with myrrh and aloes
and cassia;
Out of ivory palaces stringed instruments have made
You glad.
Kings' daughters are among Your noble ladies;

At Your right hand stands the queen in gold from Ophir.
Listen, O daughter, give attention and incline your ear:
Forget your people and your father's house;
Then the King will desire your beauty.
Because He is your Lord, bow down to Him.
The daughter of Tyre will come with a gift;
The rich among the people will seek your favour.
The King's daughter is all glorious within;
Her clothing is interwoven with gold.
She will be led to the King in embroidered work;
The virgins, her companions who follow her,
Will be brought to You.
They will be led forth with gladness and rejoicing;
They will enter into the King's palace.
In place of your fathers will be your sons;
You shall make them princes in all the earth.
I will cause Your name to be remembered in all generations;
Therefore the peoples will give You thanks forever and ever.

The way to live well on earth as in heaven is to do so without seeing the join. To live seamlessly: our feet on earth, our body in the heavens. When we say This is That, it is because we so desire that everyone sees what we see – a Creator who is with us, walking around and passing by. Our experience of the presence of God is not unreal but firmly rooted in our experience of daily living, ruling and subduing. Our daily life is charged with the grandeur of God. Both atheistic humanism and religious esotericism take us away from the anticipation that we will one day be living both in earth and in heaven. This is the Jesus way – to live a seamless existence where you can't see where one starts and the other ends, because that is not how it is any more. The two are one. Like a husband and wife, they are now one flesh, one identity, complementing and complimenting one another.

This is the picture Jesus most often uses for the Kingdom of Heaven. His return is like a bridegroom arriving to marry his bride. The experience of the Kingdom is like being invited to a wedding feast. The bringing together of lovers, the generations, family, friends, food, music, dancing, planning and purpose is all summed up in the marriage supper of the Lamb of God. The two have become one. What was lost is now found. What was once broken apart is now joined together. All power, all knowledge and all love are not three opposing attributes of an impassive immutable God. They are all summed up in what it means for God to be betrothed to his creation – animals, the earth, and of course, people. This is beautifully written by Hosea:

> *In that day I will also make a covenant for them*
> *With the beasts of the field,*
> *The birds of the sky*
> *And the creeping things of the ground.*
> *And I will abolish the bow, the sword and war from*
> *the land,*
> *And will make them lie down in safety.*
> *I will betroth you to Me forever;*
> *Yes, I will betroth you to Me in righteousness and in justice,*
> *In lovingkindness and in compassion,*
> *And I will betroth you to Me in faithfulness.*
> *Then you will know the Lord.*
> *"It will come about in that day that I will respond,"*
> *declares the Lord.*
> *I will respond to the heavens, and they will respond to*
> *the earth,*

*And the earth will respond to the grain, to the new wine
and to the oil,
And they will respond to Jezreel.
I will sow her for Myself in the land.
I will also have compassion on her who had not obtained
compassion,
And I will say to those who were not My people,
'You are My people!'
And they will say, 'You are my God!'"*[277]

---

277. Hosea 2:18-23.

This is That

The new thing is beginning, the garden is no longer at our backs with a wilderness stretching before us as it was for Adam and Eve, but the promised land is now in sight and the age of sin's dominion is now over.

When the Kingdom of Heaven breaks in, as it did on that day for the disciples, then it comes with evidence and signs. Just as Jesus was observed as God-pointing by Nicodemus, with all the Kingdom signs he was performing, so we can point and declare This is That, when the Kingdom of Heaven comes close. Of course this will be shouted when the dead rise and the blind see. But it is also to be pointed out when the heart is renewed and when the hurt is forgiven. A change of heart and attitude, a new mindset from selfishness and violence to generosity and tenderness is the most extraordinary miracle and sign of the Kingdom that could ever be. And this, too, is manifested among families, neighbours and even strangers so that whole communities become temples of Shalom. This is that, which the prophets spoke about. This is the Kingdom coming close.

So, too, is the creative pressure of subduing and the justice of ruling. So is the work of cultivating and the resilience of protecting. When the will of God is done, so this is the Kingdom.

This is that which the prophet spoke about:
when the grandparents watch the children play safely in their streets;

when the labourer is worthy of his wages and the artist colours her canvas with prophetic imagination;
where the nurtured earth nourishes and the skies drop their dew;
when the front door is open and the laughter is heard;
when the once broken heart overflows with beautifully bound books of delight;
when the kings of the earth bring the wealth of the nations inside the walls of the city;
when the crema holds the sugar and when the high voltage fluctuations are ironed out;
somewhere a human being has been subduing and ruling, cultivating and keeping.

This, is that.

Printed in Great Britain
by Amazon

61894172R00169